The Inner Child Healing Journal

A 30-Day Exercise Guide to Begin Healing Your Nervous System & Reconnect with Your Younger Self

Cody Fast

First Edition ISBN - 9798303934986

This Journal Belongs to:

_____

Date:

_____

❧ Exercise ❧
─── Guide ───

For the children.

Years ago, when I first started my healing journey, I was surrounded by such overwhelming trauma I didn't even know where to begin. Allowing myself to feel the slightest bit of emotion or talk about what I had survived would send me into a complete meltdown or chronic dissociation. On top of that, I lacked the resources to speak with a professional who could help me with all of it.

Fast forward to today, I've built a life that embodies regulation, safety, infinite self-love, and overwhelming abundance. Looking back, what I wish I had at the start of my healing journey was a foundational guide that went beyond just "mindfulness" or "talking through it."

While mindfulness techniques have their place, they can only take you so far. What's truly needed is an approach that works with the nervous system alongside inner child healing work to create lasting, sustainable healing at a subconscious level—from the body to the brain.

My goal with this journal is to build a lighthouse for anyone lost in the dark waters of overwhelming abuse, neglect, and trauma. To help guide them to that light through the storm and learn how to regulate through the waves of emotional turbulence.

To meet their inner child wherever they were first forgotten and begin fostering a deep relationship with them.

To shine a light into the darkest parts of our childhood and better understand why we are the way we are—why we react or get triggered the way we do.

To pinpoint and become aware of when we were taught to hate ourselves and, most importantly, **how to begin deconstructing that.**

...

This 30-day journal offers an exercise each day, drawing from practices I have personally used and continue to use. I've included insights from my Neuro-Somatic Intelligence training, personal breakthroughs, and lifetime experiences. You can move at your own pace or complete the journal within 30 days.

What I will say is that you must move at the pace that your inner child feels safest doing so.

This means not forcing and pushing yourself through each exercise if you are becoming significantly activated (racing heart rate, anxiety, overwhelm, the beginning of a panic attack, etc.), as doing so can potentially retraumatize you, your nervous system, and your inner child.

But first, what is an inner child?

My definition is simple.

Your inner child is where you were first forgotten, where your parents or your primary caregivers initially abandoned you. The place where you might have had to prematurely grow up because of the abuse, neglect, and overall trauma you were forced to survive. That younger you who is still living in your subconscious.

But maybe you're not even sure if you experienced trauma as a child. In my opinion, most of us have, though we may not have done enough—or any work to uncover the root causes of that trauma.

As we work through this journal, you'll gain a deeper understanding of trauma, where it stems from, and how to begin healing it through your nervous system. We'll specifically focus on nurturing your inner child and strengthening your relationship with them. As mentioned, move at a safe pace for you and your younger self.

Opening Letter

'The Forgotten Child'

I think I've lost who I was.

Or maybe I never figured out who I truly am.

Pieces of myself that I thought would join me for the rest of my life.

I think they're dying; maybe they're already dead.

Maybe that's why I'm in so much pain, or maybe I feel absolutely nothing.

Maybe that's why I'm unsure where to go next or what to do.

I'm grieving those pieces, fading away, creating more space.

Emptiness.

Maybe I feel so heavy because I feel the weight of needing to fill the space.

But what used to be there were parts of me that maybe weren't actually me.

Hopeless aspects of a fragmented self.

Fantasizing about a future where I was finally seen and loved.

To feel like I was whole.

But that's the thing with healing.

Part of the journey is this realization.

That there's never been anything wrong with you.

That there are no missing puzzle pieces.

The pieces you've been searching for your whole life.

The pieces you've asked others to give you with the hope you would finally feel like you were enough.

To finally feel whole.

But that's the thing about asking others to fill the void.

If they leave, it gets even deeper, because now they're gone, and they've taken those pieces with them.

Sending you back on the path of searching for those missing pieces once again.

The path that never ends.

Never-ending, maybe because it's trying to lead you inward.

Back to your inner self.

To the time when you were first taught that there was something wrong with you.

That you needed to set out to fix that thing.

An endless journey that ends with nothing.

Because there is nothing.

Nothing missing.

Nothing wrong with you.

The puzzle pieces are not missing.

They're simply waiting to be discovered.

Inward.

The place where the bridges were first abandoned.

Standing on the other side of those unfinished bridges is your inner child, waiting, holding their hands wide open, with those same puzzle pieces, so excited to meet and show you what they could never share with the ones who abandoned them so early on in life.

The bridges that connect present you, to younger you.

The times when you had to grow up but were still a child.

The times when people commended you for how mature you were for your age.

The times when you needed to abandon your innocent, childlike self so early on in life so that you would survive.

Survival for self, paradoxically, was where you first abandoned yourself.

That child is now inside.

They always have been.

Start to rebuild the bridges.

Show them it's safe.

Show them what safe love is.

Because now, you are safe to do so.

Begin.

<u>Day 1</u>

'The Basics and The Bridge'

The Basics

Before we begin anything, we must remember what can happen as we move through these healing exercises. As said at the beginning of this journal, if you feel activated, panicked, triggered, or overwhelmed, stop the exercise immediately and use the breathing technique you are about to learn.

New Healing Term: "Window of Tolerance"

If you are unfamiliar with this term, it is the safe or optimal zone of minimal activation in which a person can function and respond to stress in a healthy and adaptive way.

Within this window, an individual can effectively process emotions and cognitively manage challenging situations without becoming overwhelmed.

It is a term used in trauma and mental health work to describe the range of emotional intensity that a person can safely tolerate.

When a person is within their window of tolerance, they feel mostly safe and grounded, and their nervous system is in balance, typically leaning toward **parasympathetic activation (rest and digest).**

However, when a person is pushed outside their window of tolerance, they usually will experience **sympathetic activation (fight or flight)** due to a perceived threat or trauma that is still living in the body and chronically dysregulating the nervous system.

But *what is* the nervous system?

Imagine a web of nerves and strands interconnecting every organ and extremity directly up to your brainstem, firing nonstop electrical pulses of vital information to the different parts of your brain from one cluster of neural connections to another—a physiological coding of sensations and commands buzzing nonstop beneath and throughout your skin.

Your nervous system governs your perception of threats and safety, determining what is life-threatening and what is not. This process involves three distinct types of sensory input systems:

1. **Exteroception:** Responsible for external sensory inputs (vision, hearing, taste, touch, and smell)
2. **Interoception:** Internal bodily sensations/feelings/emotions and equilibrium (heart rate, respiration, visceral organs, thermoregulation, tension/relaxation, and sense of ownership)
3. **Proprioception:** Helps you understand your body's position and movement in space (3D map of your body in space & time)

At any given moment, your brain takes in around 400,000,000,000 pieces of sensory data per second—yes, 400 billion—all originating from different parts of your nervous system, sensory input systems, and body. These signals are then filtered through your various levels of perceived consciousness and unconsciousness, moving through the brainstem and other areas of the brain itself to decide what could threaten your survival and whether it needs to alert you.

A myriad of energy, electrical impulses, and emotional embodiments determining how we feel, both physically and mentally–a conduit of consciousness.

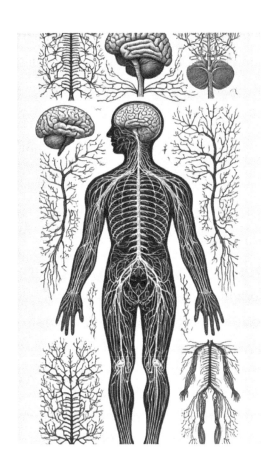

···

This breathing technique you are about to learn (also can be considered a meditation) is used to calm the nervous system out of an overly activated state and return to homeostasis.

The caveat is that this sort of breathing exercise can also be potentially triggering for some people, as trying to relax or focused breathing can also activate and overwhelm your nervous system because "relaxing" or focusing on your breathing doesn't feel safe due to past trauma.

Each nervous system is individualistic, based on our past survived experiences and trauma.

> "*Your immune cells are like a circulating nervous system. Your nervous system, in fact, is a circulating nervous system. It thinks. It's conscious.*"

—Deepak Chopra

What is Trauma?

Trauma Is:

- A **Protective Response** in the Body and Nervous System

- Causing Long-Term Dysregulation

- Overwhelms the Capacity to Cope and Adapt in Stressful or Triggering Situations

- A Physiological Response which means it's happening **INSIDE** the Body

Trauma is Not:

- The Event

- Cognitive

- The Same for Everyone

Types of Trauma:

- **Acute (Single Incident):** Natural disaster, car wreck, violent incident, death, shooting, DV, etc.

- **Chronic (Ongoing/Repeated):** Consistent stress and trauma that can happen in childhood or adulthood.

- **Complex Trauma (Ongoing):** This is **relational** trauma where escape is not possible. Often developmental, CPTSD can result from this (complex post-traumatic stress disorder).

- **Structural Trauma (Systemic):** Contextual features of environments and institutions that give rise to trauma, maintain it, and impact stress response like:

  - Educational System
  - Religion
  - Indoctrination
  - Politics
  - Medical System
  - Mental Health System
  - Law Enforcement
  - Historical/Generational Trauma
  - Body Shame
  - Racism
  - Misogyny
  - Homophobia
  - Transphobia
  - Bias
  - Socioeconomic Stress

Trauma can impact how humans relate to themselves, others, and the world, often resulting in lasting changes in behavior, mood, and thinking.

Examples of traumatic experiences include physical or emotional abuse/neglect, accidents, natural disasters, violence, and loss. Still, trauma is highly subjective—what is traumatic for one person might not be for another, depending on factors like individual resilience and support systems.

The goal of healing (especially with our inner child) is to create capacity in the nervous system (growing that window of tolerance slowly over time) for us to be able to move through the daily stressors and triggers of life with more regulation. To more effectively handle what could be sending our nervous system into a state of overwhelm.

Our nervous systems can only handle so much stress and dysregulation daily. If we are constantly being over-activated, that means our nervous system is either operating at full capacity or completely overwhelmed. Think of it like a "stress bucket."

For some of us, this stress bucket may have been overflowing for most of our childhoods, and our nervous systems were developed within that framework; they were primed for trauma responses.

In our NSI community, we say, "***What we do often, we get good at***."

If your nervous system and brain frequently default to a trauma response because of unprocessed past trauma, they're likely to continue doing so unconsciously. This is why it's crucial for trauma to be validated, processed, and released somatically through emotional regulation, crying, neuro-somatic drills, breathing, and similar modalities.

We need to remind the nervous system consistently that it is safe to process and release any residual trauma or stored emotional turmoil.

"*Trauma is not what happens to you, it's what happens inside you.*"

—Dr. Gabor Maté

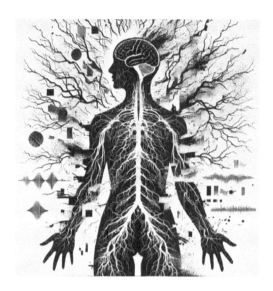

This over-activation or "threat level" within the nervous system and body can cause any number of harmful nervous system outputs that include:

- **Physical Pain (chronic/acute)**
- **Anxiety**
- **Depression**
- **Mental Disorders**
- **Inflammation**
- **Negative Thoughts & Feelings**
- **Fight/Flight/Freeze/ Flop/ Fawn**

- **Dissociation**
- **Derealization**
- **Adrenaline/Cortisol**
- **Panic Attacks**
- **Breathlessness**
- **Brain Fog**
- **Dizziness**
- **Vertigo**
- **Immobility**
- **Binge Eating**

- Substance Use & Abuse
- Self-Medicating
- Immune Dysfunction
- Hormone Dysfunction
- Insomnia
- etc.

With long-term, chronic nervous system overwhelm, we fall into the category of survival on the far end of the spectrum, where thoughts of giving up on life and self-harm may start to show up.

But over time and working within the nervous system, we can help our bodies naturally reduce these detrimental outputs and begin to have more healthy ones like:

- **Clear Thinking**
- **Regulation (physical & emotional)**
- **Presence**
- **Confidence**
- **Logical Decisions**
- **Pain-Free Movement**
- **Strength & Speed**
- **Coordination**
- **Great Balance**
- **Healthy Immune & Hormone Systems**

The Five F's

Fight, Flight, Freeze, Flop, and Fawn are the five trauma (stress) responses we commonly hear about. They are reflexive, adaptive coping mechanisms that occur whenever we experience enough perceived threat to our system.

Fight or flight is exactly how it sounds: can you *fight* the perceived threat, or can you escape it (*flight*)?

Freeze is the precursor to fight or flight because your brain is trying to determine if it can do either. If it cannot fight or flight, it will chronically remain in freeze, which is where *flop* shows up.

Flop occurs when there is no escape, leading to a shutdown response. Similar to how a possum "plays dead" as a coping mechanism, humans may experience this as chronic or acute dissociation. This can manifest as mentally checking out, losing awareness of internal felt sensations, and disconnecting from emotions completely.

It is a compounding effect often seen in individuals who have endured long-term, complex relational trauma. The longer you remain in this state, the more your internal systems begin to shut down, resulting in severely detrimental outputs from your nervous system on the far end of the spectrum of extreme overwhelm and dysregulation.

Fawn is a behavioral adaptation developed for survival. It is essentially a pattern of people-pleasing and is a learned response to mitigate perceived threats or maintain safety in relationships.

Maybe, when you were younger, you learned it was safer to remain quiet so you wouldn't upset your parent or primary caregiver.

Perhaps it felt safer to "act" happy instead of showing your authentic emotions because expressing them might have resulted in physical or verbal abuse.

Maybe you learned that love was conditional upon your achievements and had to be earned. Or perhaps you were taught that to keep people in your life, you needed to abandon your own needs in favor of theirs.

There are countless examples, but the key is to **begin repatterning our nervous systems,** fostering more regulation and safety as we navigate situations and conversations that may trigger us and lead to any of these trauma responses.

The Bridge

This exercise can be done standing or sitting, though sitting is recommended. Ensure you are in a safe, comfortable space to reduce the likelihood of over-activation.

* Please read through all the steps before starting this exercise to understand the process. *

Healing is to influence, not force. This practice communicates to your inner child, nervous system, and brain that experiences that once triggered overwhelm or shutdown can now be met with regulation and safety in the body. These new responses can help support you in navigating daily life.

Steps:

1. **Position Yourself:** Sit up straight with your spine aligned. Place one hand over your heart (either hand) and the other on your lower back, resting the back of your hand there to avoid wrist strain.

2. **Prepare to Breathe:** Keeping your hands in position, close your eyes. (If closing your eyes feels unsafe, keep them open and find a soft focus point.) Slowly inhale through your nose, visualizing your diaphragm (below your rib cage) and lungs filling with air.

3. **Exhale Slowly:** Gently release the air through your mouth, visualizing your diaphragm and lungs contracting as they empty. Continue this pattern: inhale slowly through your nose and exhale even more slowly through your mouth.

4. **Add the Word "Peace":** As you inhale, think of the word *"peace"* for the duration of your breath. Imagine the oxygen is infused with calming, revitalizing energy that soothes your nervous system, body, and brain.

5. **Add the Word "Release":** As you exhale, think of the word *"release"* for the full out-breath. Visualize any negative or stuck energy leaving your body completely.

6. **Repeat:** Perform this breathing technique for 8–10 repetitions, adjusting the duration to your comfort level or "window of tolerance."

Finding Your Window of Tolerance:

Continue until you feel your body enter a calm state—when your thoughts slow down, or you gain clarity. If calmness feels elusive, be patient. Each nervous system responds differently, and your body may need time to adjust to this practice. Offer yourself grace as you build familiarity with this exercise.

Breathing is the foundation of regulation in the body, as it happens 24/7. To maximize the benefits of this exercise, practice it daily. With consistent use of intentional breathing and the visualization of *"peace"* and *"release,"* your subconscious can begin associating these words with your natural breathing rhythm. Over time, this can help you regulate your nervous system automatically, even during life's daily stressors.

This tool will now be readily available when you feel triggered, anxious, or activated. Simply focus on your breath and repeat *"peace"* and *"release"* in your mind, wherever you are.

Full Exercise:

This exercise helps you establish an initial connection with your inner child using the same breathing method as before. **A gentle reminder:** connecting with your inner child may bring up strong emotions, including tears. This is normal. Your inner child is finally being acknowledged and allowed to safely feel what was suppressed/repressed long ago. If emotions arise, let them flow. Breathe through them and remind yourself and your inner child that it is safe to feel and release these emotions.

Steps:

1. **Position Yourself:** Use the same hand placement and breathing technique with the words *"peace"* and *"release."*

2. **Close Your Eyes & Visualize:** Picture yourself as a young child at the earliest age you can recall. Visualize this child standing in the distance. Focus on their appearance:

    o   What are they wearing?

    o   What expression do they have?

    o   What is the color of their eyes?

    o   How tall are they?

    o   How far away are they?

3. **Approach Your Inner Child:** Imagine walking toward them. When you reach them, embrace them. As you hug them, say:

- o *"I see you, and I love you."*

- o *"I will protect and support you for the rest of our existence."*

- o *"You can now fully rely on me for any of your needs*

- o *"You are safe, and you always will be."*

4. Feel free to say anything else that feels meaningful. This step is about establishing trust and letting your inner child know they can now safely communicate with you whenever they need to.

Deepening the Connection

Inner child healing is deeply personal and will look different for everyone. As your relationship with your inner child grows, they will feel increasingly safe sharing their feelings, especially as old traumas surface to be acknowledged.

You may experience intense emotions that feel disconnected from your present self—these may stem from your inner child. When this happens, use this exercise to validate their emotions and begin deconstructing what they are feeling.

While breathing and visualizing your inner child, ask them, *"What's going on?"* With time and patience, you will start to hear or sense answers as your mind and body learn to identify root causes.

Final Reminders: Offer grace to both your present and past selves, reassuring your inner child that they are safe to feel whatever emotions arise, now and in the future. Remember, this process takes time, but each step strengthens your bond and continually influences healing.

Write any thoughts, feelings, or emotions that came up for you in this exercise:

Day 2

'Timeline'

This exercise may be challenging for those with little to no childhood memory. However, with time and by validating the events of our past, we may begin to uncover suppressed or repressed traumas and memories.

You can type or write this out, but the key to this exercise is to construct a timeline starting from the earliest memory you can recall and begin identifying what happened to you and when.

The brain is designed to protect you; its primary responsibility is to keep you alive. This is why you may not remember much from your childhood—it might have been too traumatizing to process cognitively at the time.

This exercise helps create greater awareness of your past and forgotten memories, allowing your inner child to start feeling safer as you work through what happened.

Start with your earliest memory and then move on to the next. If your memories are far apart, that's completely okay. The goal is to begin constructing a timeline with the most accessible memories.

This exercise can also be ongoing. As you move through this journal, more memories may surface. Write them down and take time to reflect on them. Ask your inner child what emotions arise as you think back, recall these experiences, and make a note of them on this timeline.

You can also incorporate the breathing exercise, especially if some memories are triggering. Remember, you now have the ability to help your inner child feel safe by validating and deconstructing the overwhelming emotions connected to these memories.

It is safe now.

<u>Memory Examples for Timeline</u>

First Memory from Childhood:

First Time You Remember Feeling Joy:

First Time You Remember Feeling Unsafe:

First Time You Were Excited for Something:

First Time You Felt Guilty or Ashamed:

First Secret You Kept to Yourself:

First Crush or Best Friend:

First Dream/Hope for Your Future:

Day 3

'Safety'

This next exercise is especially important after beginning to construct your timeline of childhood memories. Now that you're focusing more attention and awareness on your past, it's crucial to help your inner child feel safe and understood as you start the healing process from your survived experiences.

We'll return to the breathing exercise, but this time, as you visualize your inner child with your eyes closed (you can keep them open to read the mantra and, once memorized, do it with eyes closed), say out loud:

"Little *[your name]*, it is safe now to begin feeling what you were never allowed to feel. Your feelings and emotions are 100% valid, and I am here to support and love you. We can now process these emotions together, as it is safe to do so. As we begin to move through and deconstruct the bigness of them, we can start to heal and release them. It is safe, and I love you so, so much."

You can use this mantra as often as you'd like. The more you practice it, the safer your inner child will feel, allowing them to validate, process, release, and eventually heal from past traumas. The main goal is to establish safety and reassure your inner child that moving through their emotions with you is okay.

You're welcome to adjust the words and phrases to make them your own in the space below:

Inner child healing relies heavily on the power of our words and thoughts when speaking to ourselves. If you find yourself talking down or saying hurtful things to yourself, ask: *"Would I say these things if I were speaking directly to my younger self?"*

Begin reframing your self-talk as though you're speaking to your inner child. You might realize how harmful your internal dialogue can be when imagining your younger self standing in front of you, especially if you have been through extensive childhood abuse and neglect.

Gentle parenting (a future exercise) is key to nurturing our inner children, especially when healing our subconscious addictions, patterns, and habits we may have developed throughout our lives.

Repeat this exercise as often as you like, but always speak with intention. With every thought and word, send love and safety to your inner child. Over time, with repetition, they will feel increasingly safe and communicate with you more often.

Day 4

'Inner Child Check-In & Neuro Tools'

This exercise ideally needs to become a daily practice, especially when you feel triggered, so that we continually strengthen our relationship with our inner child as we grow older. Your inner child never disappears; they will always be with you. However, they may mature as you heal on your journey.

The exercise is simple: whenever you feel anxious, uncomfortable, or triggered, ask your inner child, "Do you feel safe enough to do this with me?"

As we've discussed before, the more we communicate with our inner child, the safer they will feel opening up to us about how certain people, situations, and environments affect them. The goal is to live your life guided by your inner child, listening to their subtle cues about what feels safe and what doesn't.

If they don't feel safe, or you don't feel confident in your ability to protect them through an experience, you don't have to proceed. This is why establishing boundaries is so important. Many of us operate on autopilot, rarely stopping to ask if we feel safe doing something.

This often stems from a lifetime of dissociation or numbing out from our emotions.

As we continue validating, processing, and releasing the traumas stored in our bodies, we'll create more capacity to slow down and truly notice how certain experiences feel. This allows us to question, with curiosity, how our bodies respond.

People often ask, "How do you feel?"

However, many of us struggle to answer because of internal chaos or disconnection from our emotions. A more helpful question might be: "How does this show up in your body? Where do you feel it? Is it comfortable or uncomfortable to sit with?"

Once we've identified these sensations, we can introduce neuro tools to regulate the nervous system. This helps it learn that while we can handle discomfort, we only do so after ensuring our inner child feels safe. Let them know they are protected now.

Remind your inner child that they never have to do anything that doesn't feel safe because you have the agency to protect them.

What is a "Neuro Tool?"

Neuro tools are techniques or practices designed to directly influence the nervous system's physiological responses. They intentionally and repetitively activate specific brain structures, neurological pathways, and sensory input systems through neuro-targeted exercises.

The clearer and more accurate the inputs, the more predictable the outcomes, fostering a greater sense of safety within the brain. Through applied neurology, somatic exercises, and vagus nerve stimulation, we can retrain the brain to better handle and modulate through daily life stressors and triggers. This is called **neuroplasticity**—the actual rewiring of your neural networks and pathways within your brain, shaping your entire personality and how you react or respond to your perceived external reality.

With intentional doses of activation in the nervous system, we can repattern our subconscious identity and reconnect with our inner child to reparent them and influence healing.

Foundation Neuro Tools:

We will start with these first and explore how they interact with your nervous system.

When working with the nervous system, it's essential to approach each technique with curiosity and patience. Everyone's nervous system is unique, shaped by past experiences, trauma, and your window of tolerance. What feels calming and supportive to one person could be overly activating for another.

Experiment with these tools and notice how your body and mind respond. Take your time with each; remember, the goal is to find what works best for you.

Notice physical sensations (such as tension, relaxation, or warmth), emotional responses (calm, overwhelm, or joy), and mental states (clarity, fogginess, or stillness). This helps you identify patterns and determine what resonates best.

If a practice feels uncomfortable or activating, it's okay to modify it. For example, try shallower, slower breaths if deep breathing feels too intense. The key is to listen to your body's cues without judgment.

*1. Foot Sensory Stimulus *

This neuro tool is designed to help with sensory awareness and grounding by activating your **proprioceptive system** and strengthening the connection between your mind and body. This approach is especially helpful for breaking through feelings of dissociation or disconnection from yourself or your emotions. By starting at the feet and gradually moving upward, it takes a gentle, bottom-up approach that can feel less overwhelming, especially for those who have experienced chronic dissociation.

Setup:

- Choose a cloth or object that feels good (not your own skin).
- Sit or position yourself comfortably to access your feet.
- *Note:* Avoid skin-to-skin contact for this drill.

Steps:

1. Rub the entire surface of one foot with the chosen object, staying as present as possible (in a tooth-brushing motion). Notice areas with heightened or diminished sensation.

2. Close your eyes or maintain a soft gaze, imagining the part of your foot you're stimulating, including details like scars or tattoos.

3. Optional techniques:

   o Slide your fingers between the metatarsal bones (long, thin bones on the top of your foot).

   o Hold your foot with one hand on the heel and the other on the ball, gently twisting in both directions.

4. Focus on long, calm breaths (preferably through your nose) with extended exhalations.

5. Assess each foot separately, noticing any differences in sensation.

Cues to Explore:

- Can you feel the area your foot occupies in space?

- Are you aware of all parts of your foot?

- Can you create a detailed mental image of your foot with your eyes closed?

Modifications and Progressions:

- Experiment with different stimuli (e.g., vibration, sharp, hot, or cold objects).

- Adjust the duration of the stimulus.

- Practice with eyes open or closed.

- Try different body positions to vary the experience.

- Over time, you can gradually move up to your ankle, calf, knee, thigh, and so on to expand your window of tolerance.

The goal is to make this tool part of your daily routine, helping to build awareness and connection between your body and brain whenever you feel disconnected or begin to dissociate.

*2. Cranial Nerve 1 Reset *

This neuro tool is designed to enhance sensory awareness and **olfactory function** (sense of smell) while promoting safety and regulation. By focusing on your sense of smell and incorporating gentle nasal stimulation, you can improve your connection to sensory input and support nervous system regulation. This is an excellent tool for anxiety or overwhelm.

Setup:

- Choose a scent you enjoy and place the object with the scent under one nostril. Essential oils are great.

- Seal the other nostril to isolate the scent.

- Assess the scent's strength on a scale of 1 to 10 and note whether you can identify it.

Steps:

1. Smell the chosen scent while gently tapping up and down the side of the open nostril with your finger.

2. Perform 3 to 5 repetitions for the nostril.

3. Reassess the scent's strength and clarity before switching to the other side.

4. Repeat the process on the opposite nostril.

5. Focus on the nostril that provides the most positive sensory experience for further repetitions.

Cues to Explore:

- Breathe with gentle inhales and relaxed exhales.

- Close your eyes, if possible, to heighten your sense of smell.

- Use soft, light taps for stimulation.

Modifications and Progressions:

- Try different scents to explore a variety of sensory inputs.

- Adjust the number of repetitions based on comfort and effectiveness.

- Use more gentle or fewer taps for a softer stimulation.

- Experiment with different body positions to vary the sensory experience.

This tool can be customized to your preferences and training needs, providing a simple yet effective way to tune into your sense of smell and cultivate regulation through the breath.

---

3. Peace/Release Breathing

*Go back to Day 1 for full neuro tool breakdown. *

As you progress through this journal, you will be introduced to additional neuro tools designed to complement specific daily exercises. Your task is to explore these tools and identify which resonate most effectively with your nervous system. Remember, this is a personal journey, and finding what works best for you and your inner child is an essential part of the process.

---

*For a complete list of **50+ neuro tools** with demonstrations, all in a video course, where I also teach you how to assess and reassess your nervous system, go to the main link on any of my social media pages. **

Day 5

'Identify & Rewire Limiting Beliefs'

On day three, we briefly touched on negative self-talk. Today, we'll dig deeper into its root causes—exploring why we say and believe these negative things about ourselves. More importantly, we'll identify when and where we were taught these beliefs, which likely stem from the early developmental stages of childhood.

These are known as "core beliefs." They arise from our lived and survived experiences and societal, cultural, and family influences. If these core beliefs don't uplift us, foster sustainable confidence, encourage self-love, or create a sense of safety, they can be classified as **"limiting beliefs."** Limiting beliefs hold us back from reaching our full potential.

For example, suppose I subconsciously believe I don't deserve happiness in a relationship or repeatedly find myself in abusive relationships. In that case, I may hold a limiting belief that I don't deserve autonomy, safety, or unconditional love from a partner.

This is why people often struggle to change habits or transform their lifestyles. Without addressing limiting beliefs, change is difficult, and success can feel unattainable.

Similarly, when someone tries to heal, quit an addiction, or make lasting improvements, sheer willpower often isn't enough. Limiting beliefs, rooted in subconscious patterning, continue to influence and enforce behaviors, habits, and addictions. They can also lead to recurring patterns, such as ending up in similar negative situations or relationships—whether romantic, platonic, or professional.

New Healing Term: Minimal Effective Dose

The minimal effective dose is exactly as it sounds: the smallest amount of stimulus needed to engage your nervous system and bring you into the "window of tolerance" without overwhelming it or triggering a trauma response.

- **Minimal**: As little as possible.

- **Effective**: Just enough to create a new, safe experience so that your brain and nervous system learn it's okay to begin healing.

- **Dose**: The specific stimulus or exercise introduced to the nervous system.

By practicing this concept daily, you can create long-term change and healing in your thought patterns, behaviors, and subconscious core beliefs.

Part 1: Identify Belief

*Answer each question in the spaces below. *

What is the behavior, pattern, or action you want to see change in? *Example: I want to stop self-sabotaging as much as I do.*

What is the belief underneath this thing?

More often than not, we need to sit with the behavior, pattern, or action to get a deeper understanding of what is happening underneath it.

This question might take some time to answer, as you have to really sit with it and think about what the underlying belief might be. Get curious, ask your inner child questions, and see if they are communicating anything to you.

Example: I believe that I don't deserve good things.

What does the belief mean to you?

Example: If I don't deserve good things, then that means I am not worthy of them.

Part 2: Self Compassion

How has this belief protected you?

Example: Believing that I don't deserve good things has protected me from potential future disappointment if that good thing doesn't show up.

Are there ways in which the belief still protects you and creates safety for your nervous system?

Example: The belief protects me from being let down and hurt.

Can you find the space to be grateful for the belief?

Example: I am grateful for this belief because it has protected me from future disappointment because I have been let down by so many people in the past.

Part 3: Reframe

How does this belief feel in my body?

Example: This belief makes me feel invisible and not worthy of anything. Like I'll never be enough.

How does this belief constrict or limit me now?

Example: This belief keeps me from seeing things through and actually getting/experiencing that potential good thing. Sabotaging it before it even has a chance to manifest.

What else could potentially be true about that protective belief?

Example: It could be true that this protective belief isn't all bad.

What is a new possibility?

Example: A new possibility is that I don't need to self-sabotage anymore because I'm starting to believe that I do deserve good things.

Is there a space for an AND/NOW?

*Example: People will sometimes let me down and disappoint me, **AND** I am capable of handling that disappointment if it happens **NOW**.*

If you leaned into the new possibility, how would that feel in your body?

Example: That would feel scary in my body. It would feel activating. It would feel foreign as I'm very used to things going badly or assuming the worst possible outcome.

What are small actions you could take in the direction of the new belief?

*Example: I could just let it pan out instead of self-sabotaging the moment I feel like I need to. I could regulate my nervous system and practice the breathing exercise (or any neuro tools that work well with my nervous system) whenever I feel activated or worried about being potentially disappointed in the future. I can sit in the discomfort of the new action and remind myself and my nervous system that this uncomfortable feeling will eventually pass, and I'll be okay.

What change could this create for you over time?

*Example: It could create an entirely new life for me where I finally start letting good things show up and not sabotaging them before they have the chance to show up because I'm slowly starting to learn and often ask the question, "What if I do actually deserve good things? What if I am deserving of them?"

Part 4: Rewire

Take the new actions and regulate your nervous system with any of the given neuro tools to remind it that it's safe for you to move through this new experience with your developing beliefs.

Neuro Tools to Use for Belief Change:

*1. Ear Vibration *

This neuro tool helps activate the **parasympathetic nervous system** through vagus nerve stimulation, promoting relaxation and reducing feelings of stress or disconnection.

What You'll Need:

- A small vibrating object (like a Z-vibe) or your finger.

Steps:

1. Sit in a comfortable position and ensure you're in a quiet, safe space.

2. Place the vibrating object or your finger gently in the **cymba of the ear.**

3. Apply a light vibration, moving the top layer of skin delicately by using a feather-light touch, as if moving only the surface of the skin.

4. Focus on slow, gentle movements and tune in to the sensations.

5. Continue vibrating the object or moving your finger for a couple of minutes until you feel more regulated.

Modifications:

- Shorten the duration if it feels too intense or overstimulating, or increase it if it's not enough.

- Combine with other calming techniques, such as deep breathing or grounding exercises for enhanced benefits.

---

*2. Visual Reset *

This neuro tool promotes nervous system regulation by blocking visual input and combining it with deep breathing and gentle body positioning.

Steps:

1. Find a safe, stable place to sit or lie down.

2. Cover your eyes completely using a blindfold or by cupping your palms over them to block out all light.

3. Take slow, long exhales as if breathing out through a straw.

4. Relax the muscles around your eyes and let the darkness take over.

5. Maintain this practice for several minutes, focusing on your breath and the sensation of stillness.

Optional Add-Ons:

- Lie in a **resting posture** with your legs elevated at a 45-degree angle or against a wall at 90 degrees.

- Use passive tools like earplugs to minimize background noise or an abdominal belt for added grounding.

Modifications:

- If total silence feels overstimulating, allow for soft background sounds.

- Adjust the duration to suit your comfort level and gradually increase as you feel ready.

This tool is a simple yet powerful way to reset your nervous system, bringing a sense of calm and grounding whenever you feel overstimulated or disconnected.

Finally, celebrate the WIN! You are actively changing your brain and reshaping what it has been conditioned to believe about yourself.

Remember, **neuroplasticity** is the brain's ability to form new neural pathways and rewire itself based on new beliefs and intentional actions, creating entirely new experiences where old limiting beliefs once held you back. This process forms the foundation for changing the brain's structure and function in response to experiences.

Practice this exercise as often as you'd like, but always go at a pace that feels safest for your inner child.

DAY 6

'Art Therapy'

Art, in its simplest form, is expression—the unsuppressed flow of emotion moving through your body and onto the page. Sparks of creativity come to life as colors on a canvas, words on a screen, or strokes on a page. They are thoughts and feelings incarnate.

The next few pages have a variety of pieces of artwork to color in, which were created with the intention of allowing your inner child's creative energy to flow.

When finished, you are encouraged to rip the pages out, put your artwork on display, and remind your younger self how proud you are of them and that they have such a beautifully vibrant soul. Communicate to them that they can allow this creative energy to flow whenever they feel the desire to do so. You both can.

If none of these art pieces resonate with you, you are more than welcome to create your own artwork or find another source to fulfill this exercise.

The goal is to begin allowing this childlike creativity to flow daily as they feel more and more safe embodying their soul life force that may have been forgotten so long ago.

With safety, comes the capacity to embody creativity and joy, and then eventually healing.

DAY 7

'Discover Your Maladaptive Schema'

First things first, what is an Early Maladaptive Schema?

To put it simply, EMSs are deeply ingrained patterns of thinking and feeling that develop in childhood, often in response to unmet emotional needs, and continue to affect our relationships, self-esteem, and behaviors as adults.

An Early Maladaptive Schema (EMS) Test can help identify core patterns of thinking, feeling, and behavior developed in childhood that are still negatively impacting a person's life today. Below is a simplified test based on the 18 schemas originally outlined by Dr. Jeffrey Young in Schema Therapy. It consists of self-reflective questions designed to identify potential schemas.

A schema is simply a cognitive framework that helps us organize and better understand the information being presented to us, in this case, our childhood traumas.

The test is divided into different sections corresponding to schema domains (areas of unmet needs in childhood).

Each section has two statements for each schema, and for each statement, rate your agreement on a scale of 1 to 5:

1 = Strongly Disagree

2 = Disagree

3 = Neutral

4 = Agree

5 = Strongly Agree

Domain 1: Disconnection and Rejection

(These schemas relate to a belief that one's needs for security, safety, stability, nurturance, and empathy won't be met in relationships.)

1. Abandonment/Instability

☐ I worry that the people closest to me will leave or not be there when I need them.

☐ I fear that the people I love won't be there for me in the long term.

2. Mistrust/Abuse

☐ I feel that people will eventually hurt or take advantage of me.

☐ I tend to distrust others' motives or feel people are lying to me.

3. Emotional Deprivation

☐ I often feel emotionally neglected or that people don't really understand my emotional needs.

☐ I rarely feel that others care deeply about my feelings and provide comfort when I need it.

4. Defectiveness/Shame

☐ I often feel there is something inherently wrong or defective about me.

☐ If people knew the real me, they would reject me.

5. Social Isolation/Alienation

☐ I often feel like I don't fit in or that I'm different from other people.

☐ I feel disconnected from the groups or communities I'm part of.

Domain 2: Impaired Autonomy and Performance

(These schemas relate to expectations about oneself and the world that interfere with the ability to separate and function independently.)

6. Dependence/Incompetence

☐ I feel that I cannot cope well on my own without help from others.

☐ I frequently doubt my ability to handle everyday tasks independently.

7. Vulnerability to Harm or Illness

☐ I worry excessively about bad things happening to me (e.g., accidents, illnesses, financial troubles).

☐ I feel unusually vulnerable to catastrophes.

8. Enmeshment/Undeveloped Self

☐ I feel like I don't have a strong sense of self separate from the people close to me.

☐ I feel emotionally fused with others, especially family members.

9. Failure to Achieve

☐ I believe I am fundamentally inadequate and doomed to fail in achieving my goals.

☐ I feel like I am less competent than others in most areas of life.

Domain 3: Impaired Limits

(These schemas relate to difficulty respecting limits and boundaries, often resulting in difficulties with discipline, self-control, and cooperation.)

10. Entitlement/Grandiosity

☐ I believe that I deserve special treatment or privileges regardless of others' needs.

☐ I often feel rules don't apply to me or I should be able to do whatever I want.

11. Insufficient Self-Control/Self-Discipline

☐ I have trouble controlling my impulses and delay gratification.

☐ I find it challenging to stick to routines, goals, or tasks that require sustained effort.

Domain 4: Other-Directedness

(These schemas are about putting others' needs ahead of one's own in order to gain approval or maintain connections, often at the cost of one's own needs.)

12. Subjugation

☐ I often feel like I must suppress my desires or needs to avoid upsetting others.

☐ I feel forced to do things I don't want to do to avoid conflict or rejection.

13. Self-Sacrifice

☐ I often give up my own needs and wants to take care of others.

☐ I feel overly responsible for others' well-being, even at my own expense.

14. Approval-Seeking/Recognition-Seeking

☐ I rely heavily on others' approval or recognition to feel good about myself.

☐ I often change my opinions or behaviors to gain acceptance from others.

Domain 5: Overvigilance and Inhibition

(These schemas involve excessive focus on suppressing feelings, impulses, and spontaneity in favor of rigid rules and expectations.)

15. Negativity/Pessimism

☐ I focus more on the negative aspects of situations than the positives.

☐ I frequently worry that things will go wrong, even if things seem to be going well.

16. Emotional Inhibition

☐ I tend to hold back my emotions, fearing that showing feelings is a sign of weakness or loss of control.

☐ I suppress expressing anger, sadness, joy, or affection because I fear being judged or losing control.

17. Unrelenting Standards/Hyper-Criticalness

☐ I feel that I must meet very high standards in everything I do to avoid failure or criticism.

☐ I am often overly critical of myself and others, feeling that nothing is ever good enough.

18. Punitiveness

☐ I believe that people, including myself, deserve to be punished for mistakes or shortcomings.

☐ I often feel that mistakes should be harshly criticized rather than forgiven.

Scoring and Interpretation:

If you score 4 or 5 in a schema, you likely have that specific early maladaptive schema.

If you score 3 consistently, you may have some features of that schema, but it's not fully dominant in your life.

If you score mostly 1 or 2, this schema may not be a core issue for you.

Now, if you scored very high on multiple schemas and domains, that is more than okay. It's actually very normal for a lot of us, as we may have grown up in very unsafe, neglectful, and abusive environments.
Our parents or primary caregivers may have also passed down quite a bit of their own unprocessed trauma that we then also had to survive through on top of our own.

Give yourself grace and remember that you now have the agency and power to change your life and begin healing alongside your inner child.
We will be learning how to heal our EMSs in the next exercise.

DAY 8

'How to Begin *Influencing* the Healing of Schemas'

This is an essential reminder that **healing cannot be forced;** it can only be *influenced* by establishing safety, compassion, and regulation. Three things that many of us had very rarely, or maybe not at all, growing up.

Step 1. Recognize & Identify

Validate the pain or whatever emotion your inner child feels about the schema/s and give it space.

Begin to deconstruct and understand where the schema came from. Schemas often develop from unmet needs in childhood, such as emotional neglect, criticism, or inconsistent caregiving. Acknowledging these origins helps you externalize the schema, recognizing that it's a response to past experiences, **not an inherent truth about who you are.**

Step 2. Cognitive Restructuring

Schemas are often reinforced by irrational or distorted thinking patterns. To heal them, you need to challenge these patterns. Ask yourself questions like:

- "Is this belief actually true?"

- "What evidence supports or contradicts this belief?"

- "How would I view this situation if I didn't have this schema?"

*To get into even deeper healing work, use the "Identify and Rewire" exercise from Day 5 on the schema/s you want to begin healing. *

Step 3. Reframing Negative Beliefs

Begin to replace negative, self-defeating thoughts with more balanced, reality-based beliefs. This helps weaken the grip the schema has on your mind.

Practice self-compassion as you work through your schemas. Recognize that these patterns developed as a way to protect yourself in a challenging environment and that healing requires patience and kindness.

Step 4. Breaking Behavioral Patterns

Each schema is associated with a set of behaviors, such as **avoidance, overcompensation, or submission.** Healing requires identifying these behaviors and making conscious efforts to change them. For example:

- If you have a **Self-Sacrifice** schema, start setting boundaries and prioritize your needs.

- If you have a **Failure to Achieve** schema, try taking on small, manageable challenges to build a sense of competence and confidence.

Experiment with New Behaviors: Gradually expose yourself to new behaviors that challenge the schema. For instance, if you have a **Mistrust/Abuse** schema, you can experiment with trusting people in small ways while observing how safe relationships can feel different from past ones.

Step 5. Healing Through Relationships

Much of schema healing happens within safe, healthy, and secure relationships. By surrounding yourself with people who provide consistent support, validation, and love, you can rewire your experience of connection and begin to heal relational schemas (like **Abandonment**, **Mistrust**, or **Subjugation**).

Practice Vulnerability: Opening up to trusted individuals and being vulnerable can help counteract schemas rooted in fear of rejection or abandonment. Safe relationships provide corrective emotional experiences where your needs are met and your vulnerabilities are accepted.

*If you don't have any safe relationships to practice healing within, focus on your relationship with your inner child. Share how you're feeling; more often than not, the emotions you're experiencing are actually those of your inner child. Reassure them that you are now a safe space for these thoughts and feelings. *

With time, you will attract people who can also create a safe space for both you and your inner child. In the meantime, prioritize nurturing the connection between you and your inner child.

Step 6. Schema Healing is a Long Process

Schemas are deeply rooted, and often developed over many years, so healing them can take time. Progress is typically gradual, with setbacks and breakthroughs along the way. It's important to stay patient and consistent in your efforts.

Celebrate Small Wins: Recognize and celebrate the small victories along the way—whether it's setting a boundary, challenging a negative thought, or feeling more emotionally connected to yourself and others. These are signs of growth and progress.

New Healing Term: Trigger

A trigger is something that activates your nervous system, either in a detrimental or beneficial way—they're not always negative. This is why it's essential to **learn how to discern your triggers**. Over time, you and your inner child can begin to see that triggers aren't as frightening as they might initially seem.

Detrimental triggers act as yellow or red flags, like an internal alarm system going off. They signal that an experience has stirred your system enough to indicate unprocessed trauma stored somewhere in your body that needs attention and healing.

However, there can also be green flag triggers (sometimes called *Glimmers*), which are stimuli that evoke positive emotions such as joy, confidence, or hope. For example, hearing a song might trigger a memory of a happy moment and lift your mood. Recognizing these positive triggers can be a powerful way to support your healing journey.

Step 7. Anticipate Triggers

Be aware of situations or relationships that might activate your schemas. Anticipating triggers allows you to practice healthier responses rather than falling into automatic patterns. Using your breathing exercise or any of the neuro tools is key to establishing safety and regulation during said triggers.

Reaffirm New Beliefs: When schemas get triggered, remind yourself of the new, healthier beliefs you are developing. Reaffirm your sense of safety, worth, and autonomy with your inner child to counteract the schema's pull.

Take your time, be patient, and remember to hold compassion for both your younger and present self. Over time, as you continue this work, you'll begin to notice that things that once negatively triggered you no longer have the same effect. Your life and the relationships you nurture will start to reflect the inner healing you and your inner child are accomplishing.

You should be so proud of yourself—you're doing the hard work! :)

DAY 9

'Letter to My Younger Self'

This exercise is especially important after exploring our early maladaptive schemas. Revisiting old wounds can often lead to significant nervous system dysregulation, mainly if your childhood lacked emotional support and resulted in developmental trauma. Let's begin.

Step 1. Create a Safe and Comfortable Space

Find a quiet and comfortable place where you won't be disturbed. This is a reflective and emotional process, so being in a space where you feel safe is essential.

- Consider lighting a candle, playing calming music, or having a comforting object nearby.

- Close your eyes, take a few deep breaths, and begin "The Bridge" exercise to reestablish communication with your inner child.

Step 2. Set the Intention for Healing

Before you begin writing, set an intention. Tell yourself that the purpose of this letter is to offer love, understanding, and compassion to your younger self. You are writing to heal, support, and comfort the part of you that may have been wounded or neglected so long ago.

Writing Prompts for the Letter:

1. Opening the Letter

Begin by addressing your younger self. You can start with phrases like:

- "Dear little [your name],"

- "Dear [your age] year-old me,"

- "Hello, my younger self,"

2. Acknowledge the Time and Place

Mention a specific time or event in your past, or simply address your younger self at a particular age. Reflect on what they were going through and recognize the challenges they faced:

- "I know you are feeling [sad, lonely, scared, confused] right now."

- "I remember when you went through [event or situation] and how hard it was for you."

- "I see how much you've struggled with [school, family, friendships, self-esteem], and I want to talk to you about that."

3. Offer Reassurance and Validation

Let your younger self know their feelings were valid, and they deserved support and love. Express empathy and validation for their emotional experiences:

- "You didn't deserve to feel that way, and it wasn't your fault."

- "It's okay to feel [angry, sad, hurt]. Your feelings were always important."

- "You were doing the best you could with what you knew."

4. Give Them the Support They Needed

Imagine what your younger self needed to hear or receive during that time, and offer those words now:

- "I'm here for you now, and I will always listen to you."

- "You are worthy of love, and you always have been."

- "You are not alone, and I want you to know that you matter."

5. Reflect on How Far You've Come

Share with your younger self what you've learned and how you've grown. Tell them how their strength and resilience have helped you become who you are today:

- "You survived so much, and I'm so proud of you."

- "Your courage helped me become the person I am today, and I thank you for being so strong."

- "The pain you went through taught me important lessons, and now I can give you the love you always deserved."

6. Offer Comfort and Love

Imagine holding your younger self, soothing them, and giving them the nurturing they may have missed:

- "I will hold you as long as you need me to. Everything is going to be okay."

- "I love you just the way you are. You don't need to be anything other than who you are right now."

- "You are safe with me now, and I will protect you."

7. Give Them Permission to Heal

Encourage your younger self to let go of the burdens they've carried and to begin healing:

- "You don't have to carry this pain anymore."

- "It's okay to let go of the fear, guilt, or shame—you don't need it to protect yourself anymore."

- "You are free to be joyful, to love, and to live fully."

- "You don't need to be afraid of getting hurt, because I am now protecting you every step of the way."

Example of a Letter to My Younger Self:

Dear little [Your Name],

I see you there, and I know how hard things have been for you. You've been trying so hard to be strong, even when you feel scared and alone. I want you to know that it's okay to feel everything you're feeling—it's normal to be afraid when things don't make sense.

I remember when you felt like no one understood you, and you were always trying to be good enough. I know how much it hurt when people didn't see your heart. But I want you to know this: you are more than enough, just as you are. You don't have to prove yourself to anyone.

You are so brave, and you have been so strong. You've been carrying so much on your little shoulders, and I'm so sorry that you didn't get the love and support you needed and deserved. But I'm here now, and I'm going to take care of you. You don't have to do this alone anymore.

You are loved, deeply and completely. You don't have to be perfect, and you don't have to be anyone but yourself. I love you exactly as you are, and I'm so proud of the beautiful person you are becoming.

From this day forward, I promise to listen to you, to protect you, and to give you the kindness and compassion you've always deserved. You are safe now, and it's time to let go of the fear. You are free to be happy, to love yourself, and to begin living your life fully and authentically.

With all my love and gratitude,
[Your Name]

Write your letter in the space below:

This is an important reminder: these exercises may elicit emotional responses, such as breaking down in tears. The key is to allow these emotions to flow so that the energy they carry can move through your body and release somatically.

Crying is a natural parasympathetic response and a sign that you're actively engaging in the healing process.

Breathe through it, place your hand over your heart, and let it flow. It is safe to do so now.

DAY 10

'Make Time for Play'

New Healing Term: Mental Health Spectrum

This is a spectrum where we all exist, each individually moving one way or the other based on how much we have healed our unprocessed traumas still living in the body. Ideally, we want to be moving toward the right.

Surviving ⟶ Living ⟶ Thriving

Surviving	Living	Thriving
• Barely existing	• Often the start of the healing journey	• Your life begins to reflect the healing work you've done
• Experiencing many detrimental nervous system outputs	• Beginning to slowly feel emotions & bodily sensations	• Good days start to outweigh bad days
• Very little to no joy	• Finding more moments of joy & inspiration	• Your nervous system is often regulated
• Likely experiencing thoughts of wanting to give up on life	• Life might start feeling like it's worth it	• You're gaining more capacity to embody emotional frequences like joy and safety
• Extremely dysregulated & often disconnected from one's body & emotions	• Hope is growing	• Flowing, not forcing
	• Trust & love in self is growing	

Joy, excitement, happiness, fulfillment, passion, and euphoria—these "feel-good" emotions are among the most beautiful parts of being alive. Yet, for many of us, this side of the Mental Health Spectrum may feel almost foreign. Long-standing patterns of chronic dissociation or feeling "numbed out" from reality can make these emotions feel distant or completely non-existent.

Often, dissociating becomes our mind's safest way of coping, especially when we've faced ongoing trauma where we could not escape (flight trauma response) or fight back (fight trauma response) to protect ourselves.

It's entirely normal for our body, brain, and nervous system to shift into the protective "freeze" response to survive said trauma. Over time, and with repeated experiences and exposure, this trauma response can become deeply ingrained. Our nervous system gets "stuck," remaining numbed out and highly disconnected from our body's internal sensations and emotional embodiments.

At the furthest reaches of this spectrum, conditions like **derealization or depersonalization** can occur, where we may feel entirely disconnected from ourselves as if our body or reality isn't truly ours.

If we are not allowing the flow of ALL our emotions, we will not be able to feel the best ones we're meant to. **To heal, is to begin feeling.**

These exercises are designed to allow us to begin reconnecting with the felt sense of joy that our inner child may have had to abandon so long ago.

Start small and look to where the little you is leading present you.

1. Art and Craft Play

- **Finger Painting or Drawing**: Engage in free, unstructured painting or drawing using vibrant colors without worrying about the outcome. Allow yourself to express feelings and ideas from your inner child.

- **Collage Making**: Cut out pictures from magazines and create a collage representing what makes your inner child feel happy, safe, or heard. This playful form of creative expression can give insight into unspoken emotions.

2. Imaginative Play

- **Create a Fantasy World**: Using toys, miniature figurines, or simply your imagination, build a small world or scene. This activity encourages creativity, and revisiting childlike wonder can offer a safe space to confront emotions from the past.

- **Storytelling**: Write or verbally tell a story where the protagonist (a child version of you or an imagined character) overcomes a challenge. This allows for emotional processing and gives the inner child a voice.

3. Physical Play

- **Climbing** - Try climbing trees, playground equipment, or even indoor rock climbing to relive that sense of adventure.

- **Jump Rope or Double Dutch** - Find a rope and jump, adding chants or songs for extra nostalgia.

- **Roller Skating or Biking** - Dust off a pair of skates or hop on a bike to feel the wind on your face.

- **Jumping on a Trampoline or Swinging**: Physically playing like you would have as a child—jumping on trampolines, swinging at a playground—can be a form of release, offering a sense of freedom and fun while reconnecting with carefree moments of the past.

4. Game-Based Play

- **Board, Card, or Console Games**: Play a favorite type of childhood game by yourself or with friends. Approach the game with the lightheartedness you would have as a child, focusing on fun over competition.

- **Hide and Seek or Tag**: Engaging in classic childhood games like hide and seek, tag, or even hopscotch can reconnect you with simpler times and give you space to let go of adult stresses.

5. Nature Play

- **Building a Sandcastle or Playing with Mud**: Get your hands dirty by building a sandcastle, playing with mud, or stacking rocks. The tactile nature of these activities encourages playful reconnection with your inner child's curiosity about the natural world.

- **Cloud Watching or Stargazing**: Lie on your back and watch the clouds or stars, imagining shapes and stories. This activity connects with the wonder and imagination of childhood, inviting feelings of awe and calm.

6. Sensory Play

- **Playing with Kinetic Sand or Slime**: Engage your senses by touching, molding, and shaping kinetic sand or slime. These textures can evoke childhood sensory play and offer calming, grounding effects.

- **Bubble Blowing**: Blowing bubbles can bring back joyful memories and stimulate feelings of wonder and relaxation. Watch them float away, visualizing stress or past emotional wounds being released with each bubble.

Each form of play offers a pathway to reconnect with your inner child, fostering healing by creating space for emotional exploration, joy, and self-compassion.

These are just a few examples to try out—there are endless options to explore. The goal is to discover which activities of "play" resonate most with your inner child. Remember, trial and error is part of the process, and you can add any of your own forms of play to this list.

DAY 11

'Video Journals'

This next exercise is a video journaling practice designed to foster a compassionate dialogue with your inner child by processing emotions, daily struggles, stressors, and triggers.

By speaking directly to your inner self each day (or whenever you need to brain dump), you'll gain greater insight into your own emotional landscape, reconnect with your inner child, and work toward healing past wounds.

Why Video Journaling?

Speaking to yourself in a video format allows for an intimate, expressive outlet. Watching yourself later gives you the chance to view your emotions with compassion and understanding, which mirrors the nurturing presence your inner child may have needed. This practice fosters a sense of continuity between your adult self and your inner child, allowing for emotional processing that is both deep and affirming.

Step 1. Create a Comfortable, Private Space

Set up a comfortable, private space where you can record. Make sure you feel safe and won't be interrupted. This should be a place where you can speak freely, say whatever is currently on your mind, and brain dump.

Step 2. Choose Your Equipment

Use a device you're comfortable with—your smartphone, tablet, or laptop. Aim for a comfortable viewing angle that feels like a conversation with yourself or even setting it down if you don't want your face on the screen, whatever feels safest.

Step 3. Set an Intention for Each Session

Before you begin recording, take a few deep breaths and set an intention. This might be something like, "Today, I want to explore what's been weighing on me," or "I want to understand why I reacted so strongly to a certain situation." Setting an intention can help focus the session, making it more purposeful and meaningful.

1. Begin with a Check-In

Start each video by checking in with your current state of mind and body. You might say:

1. "Right now, I feel…"

2. "My body feels…"

3. "What's on my mind today is…"

2. Acknowledge Any Triggers or Stressors

Reflect on any situations that may have caused stress, sadness, anger, or frustration. Describe these events as if you were explaining them to a friend. Try not to judge yourself or rationalize your reactions. Simply acknowledge how you felt in that moment.

Example:

1. "Today, I felt really triggered when…"

2. "I noticed myself getting frustrated when…"

3. Talk

The goal is to speak freely about whatever comes to mind—sharing, venting, and allowing yourself to have no filter. Let your emotions and thoughts flow naturally. This process helps create more capacity in your brain, so over time, you'll feel less overwhelmed by your thoughts.

On a deeper level, this practice helps create a safe dialogue with your inner self, allowing your thoughts and emotions to be expressed verbally, giving your inner child a voice.

This release may bring about powerful emotional reactions, so it's essential to be prepared. Let these emotions flow, and give yourself and your inner child permission to fully feel whatever is demanding to be felt.

4. End with Self-Compassion

End each video by reminding yourself that your emotions are valid and normal. Affirm to yourself that you're proud of doing the work, even when it's hard, and remind your inner child that you're always there for them.

Example:

1. "Thank you for sharing this with me today. It's okay to feel these things."

1. "I'm here for you, I love you, and I'm so proud of you for speaking up about these feelings."

After Recording: Reflect & Review

1. **Watch When You Feel Ready**

   Playback can help you view yourself from a nurturing perspective. Approach it with a mindset of acceptance and curiosity rather than criticism. Try to imagine your inner child watching the video with you, encouraging understanding and support.

2. **Journal (Optional)**

   If you'd like, keep a written journal alongside your videos. Document insights, patterns, or changes in how you view yourself. This written reflection can reinforce the work done in your video journaling.

3. **Reflect on Changes in Awareness**

   Over time, you may start to notice patterns in your triggers, reactions, and self-talk. This can be empowering as you become more aware of how past wounds show up in daily life, and it opens doors for healthier emotional responses.

Tips for Success

- **Get into a Routine**: When you feel overwhelmed, pull out your recording device, hit record, and start talking.

- **Accept Imperfection**: Allow yourself to fumble or feel awkward. The goal is to be honest, not polished.

- **Practice Patience**: Healing is a gradual process. Each video journal brings a new opportunity to connect and support your inner child.

- **Celebrate Small Wins**: Notice moments when you respond differently to triggers or feel a bit more compassionate toward yourself. Recognize this progress as evidence of healing.

Final Note

Video journaling gives you the opportunity to record your in-the-moment feelings—especially those you didn't have the chance to process earlier in the day or when you initially felt overwhelmed or triggered. For those of us with complex developmental trauma, this can be an invaluable tool for beginning to deconstruct patterns and subconscious behaviors.

Over months and years of practicing video journaling, you'll be able to look back and reflect on who you used to be. You'll notice how much you've changed, particularly in how you now respond to stressors and triggers rather than overreacting emotionally.

Long-term healing begins with small, incremental changes to your lifestyle, focused on fostering greater regulation and safety as you navigate life alongside your inner child.

DAY 12

'Photo Memory Recall'

Today's exercise centers on connecting with your younger self by revisiting photographs from your childhood. If you don't have any photos on hand, don't worry—simply recall memories as best as you can. This exercise is all about deepening compassion, curiosity, and connection with your inner child.

Step 1. Prepare Your Space

Find a comfortable, quiet place where you feel safe and at ease. If you have a favorite candle, a cozy blanket, or soothing music, feel free to bring those in to make the experience more relaxing.

Step 2. Gather Photographs or Recall Memories

Choose a few photographs from different stages of your childhood. Ideally, select ones that resonate with you—whether they bring up happy, sad, or neutral feelings. If you don't have photos, close your eyes and picture yourself at a young age. You might choose specific ages or simply let memories of different moments arise.

Step 3. Observe and Reflect

Look at each photograph or hold each memory in your mind, focusing on the emotions and energy of your younger self.

Ask yourself the following questions as you look at each photo or think of each memory:

- *How does this version of me look?* Notice facial expressions, body language, and what they might be feeling.

- *What was I going through at this time?* Was this a time of joy, a challenge, or something in between?

- *What did I need most at this age?* Try to sense what that version of you might have wanted in terms of love, attention, or support.

Spend a few minutes with each image or memory, noticing any emotions that arise without judgment. If feelings like sadness, joy, nostalgia, or longing arise, allow yourself to feel them fully.

Step 4. Engage with Your Younger Self

In this step, imagine speaking to this younger version of you as if you were right beside them, offering kindness and love. You might say things like:

- *"I see you, and I know what you're going through."*

- *"You are so special, and you deserve love and happiness."*

- *"I am here for you now, and I will always be here to support you."*

- *"It's okay to feel how you feel. You are safe with me."*

Feel free to say whatever words feel right to you. This is a chance to offer yourself the support you may have needed during that time.

Step 5. Journal About the Experience

Take a few minutes to write down anything that came up during this exercise. Consider:

- Which photographs or memories were most impactful?

- What emotions did you feel, and where did you feel them in your body?

- What did you learn about your inner child?

- What kind of support, love, or encouragement did you offer your younger self?

Write your answers in the space below:

Step 6. Close with Gratitude

Finally, place a hand over your heart and thank yourself for taking this time to connect with your inner child. You've just created a moment of healing and growth; each time you do this, you strengthen the bond with your younger self.

You may want to return to these photos or memories again whenever you need a reminder of where you've been and how far you've come.

This exercise can help deepen your relationship with your inner child, allowing them to feel seen, valued, and supported. It's a powerful reminder that your past selves are always a part of you and that you now have the strength to offer them the love and acceptance they need.

DAY 13

'Boundaries'

Setting boundaries can sometimes trigger sympathetic nervous system activation, which manifests as feelings of anxiety, tension, or any of the F trauma responses.

This exercise will help you identify your boundaries, practice setting them with a regulated nervous system, and use neuro tools to regulate both before and after boundary-setting moments. Teaching your nervous system that it's safe to set boundaries is a transformative skill that allows your inner child to feel protected and secure in relationships.

Step 1. Define and List Your Boundaries

- **Journal Prompt**: Take a few minutes to write about the areas in your life where boundaries are needed to protect your inner child. List boundaries in the space below that are **non-negotiable** (those essential to your emotional safety) and **negotiable** (those that you can adjust in healthy relationships).

- **Examples:**
    - Non-negotiable: "I will not tolerate verbal disrespect."
    - Negotiable: "I need personal time each week but can be flexible on when."

Non-Negotiable:

Negotiable:

Step 2. Prepare with Regulation Tools

Use the neuro tools we previously learned that worked best with your nervous system to ground yourself before discussing or setting these boundaries. Activating the parasympathetic nervous system prepares you to communicate calmly and assertively rather than defensively. This preemptive practice is key in supporting your nervous system through boundary-setting situations.

Step 3. Setting the Boundary with Confidence

During the boundary-setting moment, use regulation tools to stay calm and prevent escalation of the sympathetic nervous system. Boundaries set with regulated confidence are often more easily accepted by others and feel more grounded to you.

Tools to Try While Communicating:

- **Mindful Breath Pausing:** Take a deep breath after each sentence to keep yourself centered.

- **Visualize a Safety Bubble:** Imagine a comforting bubble around you, protecting you and your inner child as you speak.

- o **Internal Anchor Phrases:** Use an anchor phrase such as "I am safe" or "My needs are valid" if you feel triggered.

Step 4. Post-Boundary Regulation Practice

After setting the boundary, give your nervous system another dose of healthy stimulus to regulate. This reinforces to your brain and body that it is safe to establish boundaries.

Neuro Tools to Use for Boundaries:

1. Vocal Toning

This neuro tool uses vocal toning to release tension and regulate the nervous system through the vagus nerve for **parasympathetic activation**. It also builds self-awareness and comfort with vocal expression, especially when setting boundaries.

Setup:

- Find a comfortable space where you feel safe to use your voice freely.

- Sit upright in a comfortable posture or lie down if you feel self-conscious or if sitting upright feels intimidating.

Steps:

1. Inhale Deeply: Take a slow, deep breath.

2. Vocal Exploration:

   - While slowly exhaling, begin to hum or make a sound starting as **low** as you can.

   - Gradually **move up the scale** to as high as you can.

- Focus on smooth transitions between notes.

3. Repeat 3-5 Times:

- As you repeat, bring attention to any "sticky" parts (notes that feel hard to hit or strained).

- Breathe into these spots, gently working through them with focus.

- Aim for **at least 2 minutes** of continuous sound exploration.

Modifications & Progressions

1. Simplified Approach:

   - Simply make any sound for 2 minutes without worrying about pitch or scale.

2. Expressive Play:

   - Experiment with different voice ranges:

     - Speak or hum in your **highest** voice.

     - Speak or hum in your **deepest** voice.

   - Try mimicking other tones or voices (e.g., cartoon characters, accents).

3. Advanced Exploration:

   - Exercise the **end ranges** of your voice, pushing boundaries gently.

   - Stack this exercise with other tools (e.g., grounding techniques or body movement) for deeper integration.

Key Benefits:

- Unlocks vocal tension linked to stored emotions.

- Helps with nervous system regulation and parasympathetic activation.

- Builds confidence in vocal expression.

Pro Tip: Embrace curiosity and playfulness—it's okay to sound silly!

---

2. Whole Body Mapping

This neuro tool promotes nervous system regulation and body-mind connection through the **Somatosensory Cortex** to explore and map physical sensations. It can also help in emotional processing, trauma integration, and building a sense of safety in the body.

Setup:

1. Comfortable Position:

   o Choose a position that feels comfortable (standing, sitting, or lying down).

2. Optional Object:

   o Select a sensory object (e.g., soft brush, textured fabric, or tapping tool) for external stimulation.

Cues for Success:

- No Skin-on-Skin Contact: Use a tool or object instead of hands directly on the skin to prevent overstimulation.

- Avoid Pain: If you encounter discomfort or pain, skip that area.

- Relaxed State: Maintain a calm and gentle approach throughout the exercise.

Steps:

1. Begin at the Feet:

   o Start at your feet and gradually work your way up the entire body.

   o Use your chosen stimulus (rubbing, tapping, or brushing) to explore each area.

2. Focus on Key Areas:

   o Pay special attention to tattoos, scars, or areas of emotional significance, as they often hold deeper sensations.

3. Duration:

   o Take your time with each section, moving mindfully to avoid rushing.

Modifications & Progressions:

1. Adjust Body Position:

   o Lying down: Use this position to reduce stimulation and increase relaxation.

   o Standing: Engage in this position for a more active and stimulating experience.

2. Explore Variations of Stimulus:

   o Experiment with different objects (soft brush, textured ball, tapping tool).

o Try altering the speed of the movements (slow and gentle vs. brisk and stimulating).

3. Sensory Play:

   o Practice with **eyes open** and **eyes closed** to notice the difference in awareness and sensations.

Key Benefits:

- Enhances sensory awareness and self-regulation.

- Fosters a deeper connection with the body, especially areas with past trauma or emotional significance.

- Establishes safety and regulation through intentional touch.

Pro Tip: Approach this tool with curiosity, viewing it as an exploration rather than a task to complete.

Step 5. Handling Pushback on Boundaries

If someone challenges your boundary, you may feel a sympathetic response again. When this happens, pause and use a regulation tool to calm yourself before responding. Over time, this practice trains your nervous system to feel safer each time you protect your boundaries and speak up for present you, and little you.

Quick Neuro Tools for Boundary Pushback Moments:

   o **Box Breathing (4-4-4-4):** Inhale for 4 counts, hold for 4, exhale for 4, and hold for 4. This exercise engages the parasympathetic response.

- Cold Exposure (if available): A quick cold splash on your face can activate the vagus nerve, influencing regulation.

- Self-Compassion Reminders: Remind yourself, "This boundary is here for my well-being. I'm safe, and I can handle this."

Reflect on how each step reinforced safety and well-being for your inner child. Notice if you feel a greater sense of confidence, calm, and protection each time you establish a boundary. This process of teaching safety to your nervous system is crucial for long-term healing and sets you up to thrive with healthy boundaries.

This approach integrates nervous system regulation with each aspect of boundary-setting, helping reinforce that you can feel safe while maintaining your boundaries, even in challenging situations.

DAY 14

'Mirror Affirmations'

This exercise is a powerful morning ritual designed to imprint positive beliefs into the subconscious. Upon waking, the brain is in a highly suggestible state, experiencing both **theta and alpha brain waves**– ideal for subconscious reprogramming.

In this state, your mind is naturally more open to absorbing new ideas, making it the perfect time to focus on healing, manifestation, and self-love.

Step 1. Choose Your Affirmations

Think of words or phrases that support what you want to feel and believe. These can range from feelings of self-worth and peace to deeper goals you wish to manifest. Examples could include:

- "I am deserving of self-love and respect."

- "I am Love, I am Light, I am Peace."

- "I am capable, worthy, and deserving of success."

You can also phrase your affirmations as if you're speaking directly to your younger self:

o   "You are Love, You are Light, You are Joy."

o   "You are deserving of abundance."

o   "You are new, and you are healing."

o   "It is safe for you to feel."

o   "You are not alone."

Step 2. Write on the Mirror

Use a dry-erase marker to write these affirmations on your bathroom mirror. Placing them here ensures they are among the first things you see in the morning.

Step 3. Absorb the Words

Each morning, take a moment to look at these affirmations. Say them aloud if possible, allowing yourself to feel the impact of each word. This helps to bridge the subconscious with conscious intention, allowing your inner child to feel heard, valued, and supported.

Step 4. Repeat Consistently

Daily repetition helps these affirmations become more embedded, creating a gradual shift in how you perceive yourself and your experiences.

Step 5. Reflect and Adjust

Periodically, reflect on how you feel about the affirmations. Adjust or add new phrases that resonate with any evolving needs or goals of your inner child.

By reinforcing these positive messages each morning, you create a safe, nurturing space for your inner child, helping to dissolve old, limiting beliefs and replace them with self-compassion and encouragement.

DAY 15

'Reclaiming Childhood Wishes'

Why This Exercise Matters:

Many of us carry the echoes of things we wanted as children but didn't receive. These wishes might have been simple, like wanting more time to play and be free, or more complex, like needing to feel safer, more seen, or unconditionally loved. By acknowledging these unmet wishes, you open a path to self-compassion, understanding, and healing.

Step 1. Creating a Safe Space to Reflect

Begin by finding a quiet, comfortable spot where you won't be disturbed. If you feel comfortable, you may want to close your eyes, take a few deep breaths, and imagine yourself as a child. Visualize where you spent much of your time, like your childhood bedroom, a favorite park, or a family member's home. Focus on this image until you feel connected to your younger self.

Step 2. Reflect on Childhood Needs & Wishes

Now, gently ask yourself:

- "What did I wish for as a child that I didn't receive?"

- "What did I need the most but felt was out of reach?"

Think broadly here, considering both tangible and intangible wishes. Some examples could be:

- **Physical things:** toys, new clothes, more food options, a specific gift.

- **Emotional needs:** unconditional love, approval, validation, compassion, safety, being seen.

- **Experiences:** more time to play, freedom, a sense of stability, family gatherings, being included, physical touch (hugging, cuddling, holding hands) to establish a safe and secure bond with a parent or primary caregiver.

Spend a few moments letting these memories come up naturally. There's no need to rush. Let whatever arises feel welcome, whether a small, specific wish or a deeper need.

Step 3. Writing Out Your Childhood Wishlist

In the space on the next page, start by writing a title, such as *My Childhood Wishlist.* Now, begin listing these unmet wishes and needs. You might write them out like a letter to your younger self or simply jot them down as bullet points. Allow your thoughts to flow freely and honestly.

Here's a prompt to get you started:

"Dear Younger Me, I know you wanted a lot of things that didn't come true back then. I remember that you wished for... [list out each wish as it comes to you]."

As you write, pay attention to any emotions that arise. You might feel sadness, anger, longing, or even peace as you connect with these memories. Accept these feelings as part of your journey and let the energy flow.

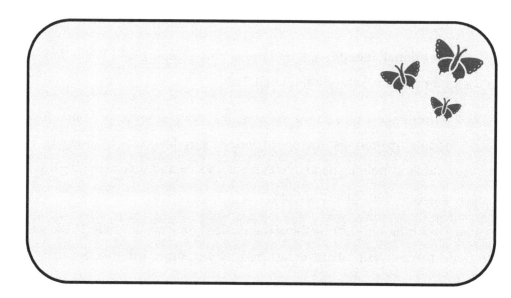

Step 4. Acknowledging & Comforting Your Inner Child

Take a few moments to speak to your inner child. Reassure them that they were not wrong to have these wishes and that it's okay they didn't receive everything they wanted. Here's a suggestion for what you could say:

"I'm here now, and I see and honor all the things you wished for. I'm sorry that some of those needs went unfulfilled. I understand you wanted... [restate a few wishes]. I'm here to listen to those needs now, and I will help you feel loved, safe, and seen."

You can add any words of encouragement or love that feel meaningful. Take your time with this.

Step 5. Creating a Present-Day Wishlist for Your Inner Child

To bring a sense of healing to these memories, create a new list—a "present-day wishlist" for your inner child. Think of small, doable ways you can meet these needs today. Here are some examples:

- **If you wanted more love and attention:** Schedule a weekly "self-care" date where you do something you love, like painting, cooking, or watching a favorite movie. Or take yourself out on an actual solo date, but imagine your inner child is joining you.

- **If you wanted a sense of stability and safety:** Create a comfortable corner in your home or space that is warm and cozy with items that make you feel safe, like a blanket, a journal, or meaningful objects. The goal is to promote the feel-good chemicals in your brain so that your nervous system learns to be more comfortable embodying safety and rest.

- **If you wished for adventure and fun:** Plan a small adventure or trip that lets your inner child explore and play, such as visiting a new place or maybe taking a fun class.

Write in the space below a few things that you can realistically bring into your life now to nurture your inner child's wishes:

Step 6: Closing Your Practice

Take a few deep breaths, and if you feel comfortable, place a hand on your heart as a gesture of self-compassion. Thank yourself for revisiting these memories and being open to healing.

End by saying to yourself:

"I am here for you. Your wishes are seen, valued, and worthy of being fulfilled in whatever ways are possible now."

Reflection:

When you're ready, write down any final thoughts or feelings from this exercise. Consider journaling below about how reconnecting with these wishes made you feel and if any actions feel particularly comforting to take forward.

Remember: This exercise is about honoring your inner child and giving them the love, recognition, and support they deserve. With time, you may find more ways to fulfill these wishes and build a nurturing relationship with your inner self.

DAY 16

'Gentle Parenting'

As mentioned on day three, a lot of us never had parents or primary caregivers that we felt safe with because we did, in fact, experience abuse that may have been verbal, emotional, mental, spiritual, or physical. Or perhaps we experienced all of them.

Practice gentle, compassionate self-talk during moments of stress, anxiety, or overwhelm to help regulate your emotions and reassure your inner child. This exercise can be done anytime and is designed to help you respond to challenging situations rather than overreacting emotionally.

Step 1. Pause and Acknowledge Your Feelings

When you notice yourself feeling upset, anxious, or overwhelmed, pause for a moment. Recognize the feeling without judgment—simply say to yourself, "I am feeling (upset/anxious/overwhelmed) right now, and that's okay."

Step 2. Take a Grounding Breath

Inhale deeply for a count of four, hold for two, and exhale slowly for a count of four. This breath can help settle your nervous system, signaling that it's safe to calm down.

Step 3. Visualize Your Inner Child

Imagine your younger self standing before you, perhaps feeling the same emotions you're experiencing. Picture them as vulnerable, innocent, and in need of comfort. Recognize that part of what you're feeling now might be coming from this child within, who may be triggered by the stress or fear of the moment.

Step 4. Speak Gentle, Kind Words Aloud or in Your Mind

Speak to your inner child in a soft, gentle voice as if you were comforting them directly. Some phrases to try include:

- "It's okay to feel this way; I'm here with you."
- "I know this feels big right now, but we can handle it together."
- "You are safe. I won't let anything bad happen to you."
- "You don't have to carry this alone."
- "I'm proud of you for feeling your feelings. You're doing great."

Use phrases that feel natural to you, adjusting the tone to be soothing, warm, and supportive. Let the words wrap around you, creating a buffer from stress.

Write them below:

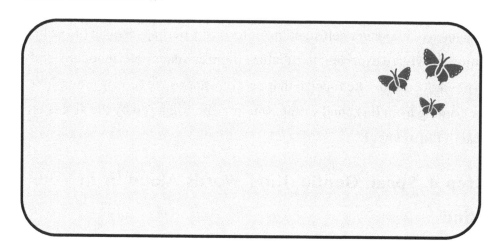

Step 5. Place a Hand Over Your Heart While Speaking to Them (Optional)

Place your hand over your heart or another comforting spot, like your stomach. This physical gesture can help reinforce feelings of safety and connection. Visualize the warmth of your hand as reassurance for your inner child as you speak the words to them.

Step 6. Allow Space for the Emotion to Pass

Gently remind yourself that emotions are temporary. You might say, "This feeling will pass," or "We can stay with this feeling without being overwhelmed by it." Allow yourself to simply sit with the emotion, giving it room to exist without needing to "fix" it right away.

Step 7. Encourage Gratitude and Self-Validation

Before moving on, say something kind and affirming, like, "Thank you for being brave enough to feel this," or "I'm so proud of you for caring for yourself." This acknowledgment reinforces that your feelings are valid and worthy of attention.

Step 8. Repeat as Needed

Use this practice as often as necessary throughout the day. Each time you respond gently to stress, you're building a habit of kindness toward yourself and creating a safe space for your inner child to express and be heard.

This soft parenting approach encourages you to meet daily stressors with gentleness rather than reactivity, fostering resilience and self-acceptance over time.

With regular practice, you will find that you can more easily self-regulate, creating a growing sense of inner peace in moments that used to feel overwhelming.

DAY 17

'Anger'

We talked about gentle parenting in our last exercise, and today, we will focus on anger. More specifically, how to process and better understand anger and release it in a healthy way.

More often than not, anger is a secondary emotion that is covering up something going on beneath it.

To explore anger as a secondary emotion, uncover its underlying causes, and deconstruct it, we will use our neuro tools for emotional regulation and to continue healing your inner child.

Step 1. Pause and Observe

When you feel anger rising, pause. Take a deep breath and acknowledge the emotion by saying out loud or in your mind, "I feel angry right now."

The purpose of this is that it creates space between the trigger and your reaction, allowing you to approach the emotion with curiosity rather than judgment.

Step 2. Identify What's Beneath the Anger

Ask yourself these reflective questions and journal or voice your responses:

1. **Was a boundary crossed?**

2. **Do I feel something is unfair or unjust?**

3. **Am I masking fear, sadness, shame, or hurt?**

4. **Is this anger directed at someone, or am I angry with myself?**

Anger often serves as a protective shield for deeper emotions. By identifying the root cause, you empower yourself to address the underlying issue.

Step 3. Regulate

Use any neuro tools that work well with your nervous system to regulate and help it understand that although these feelings are big and maybe overwhelming, it is safe to process them now. Here are a few quick ones:

1. **Deep Breathing**
   - Inhale deeply through your nose for 4 seconds, hold for 4 seconds, exhale for 6 seconds. Repeat 3–5 times.
   - **Why:** This engages the parasympathetic nervous system, reducing the fight-or-flight response.

2. **Butterfly Hug or Self-Hold**
   - Cross your arms over your chest and tap alternately on your shoulders gently.
   - **Why:** This calms the nervous system and offers a sense of safety, reassuring your inner child.

3. Grounding Technique

- o Identify 5 things you can see, 4 you can touch, 3 you can hear, 2 you can smell, and 1 you can taste.

- o **Why:** Redirecting your focus to the present moment helps de-escalate overwhelming emotions.

Step 4. Validate Your Anger

Say to yourself out loud:

- "It's okay to feel angry. Anger is a signal that something needs attention."

- "I am allowed to express my emotions safely."

If you don't validate anger, it may be suppressed or repressed internally, leading to resentment or self-blame. By acknowledging, honoring, and giving it space to exist, you teach your inner child that it's not a "bad" feeling but simply an emotion that needs to be released in a healthy way.

Step 5. Express Anger Safely Through Somatic Release

1. Punch a Pillow

- o As the name suggests, punch a pillow as many times as you need to release your anger.

- o If you want to take it a step further, say affirmations out loud while punching to combat negative thoughts, such as:

    1. "You are not ugly."

    2. "You are not a failure."

3. "You are not stupid."

4. "You are not worthless."

5. "You are not unlovable."

- ○ Feel free to use any affirmations that resonate with you. The key is to start somatically releasing the anger or pain tied to these limiting beliefs. Saying "you" instead of "I" rewrites the narrative, allowing you to detach from these negative beliefs and step into a higher version of yourself.

2. Throw It

- ○ Gather or purchase some stuffed animals or toys, and find a wall you can safely throw them at. Channel your pain and anger, releasing it with each throw. Don't hold back—use all your strength. This is a safe and constructive way to let it all out.

3. Vigorous Physical Activity

- ○ Engage in activities like running, weightlifting, or any form of physical exercise to release pent-up energy somatically. Incorporating this into your daily or weekly routine can be a powerful way to maintain emotional balance and release tension.

4. Somatic Wall Push

- ○ Position yourself facing a wall, table, or any stable surface. Ensure stability to generate force safely.

- ○ Press your hands into the surface with as much force as you can.

- ○ Hold the push briefly, then relax your body.

- o **Cues to Enhance the Experience:**
  - i. Visualize yourself creating or reinforcing a strong boundary.
  - ii. Allow natural vocal sounds or words to emerge if that feels right.
  - iii. Let your body relax, shake, or rest as needed to integrate the release.
- o **Modifications & Progressions:**
  - Alternate surfaces: push against a desk, grip and release a chair, or press into the floor.
  - Adjust intensity based on your energy and capacity—this exercise is flexible for all postures and strength levels.

5. **Rage Room**
   - o If you're ready to release years—or even a lifetime—of anger and pain, rage rooms are an excellent option for obvious reasons.

Step 6. Reaffirm Your Boundaries

If your anger stemmed from a boundary violation:

- Reaffirm the boundary by stating it calmly but firmly, e.g., "I need [space, time, or respect], and I won't accept [specific behavior]."

- Purpose: Setting boundaries reinforces your self-worth by alchemizing that anger into positive action to protect your inner child.

Step 7. Reflect and Reconnect with Your Inner Child

Sit quietly and visualize your younger self. Imagine them sitting beside you, watching you handle the anger in a healthy way. Speak to them:

- "I hear you. It's okay to feel upset. I'm here to protect you."

- Purpose: This practice helps build trust with your inner child, showing them that their emotions are valid and manageable.

Why Anger Needs Understanding, Not Avoidance:

Anger often signals unmet needs, injustice, or suppressed emotions. Beneath it, you might find:

- **Boundary violations:** Feeling disrespected or unsafe.

- **Sadness or grief:** Mourning a loss or unmet expectation.

- **Fear:** Anxiety about potential harm or failure.

- **Shame:** Feeling unworthy or judged.

By addressing these roots with compassion and regulation techniques, you move closer to healing and self-empowerment.

DAY 18

'Forgiveness & Shame'

"You need to forgive yourself in order to start healing."

We hear this often, but what does it truly mean, and how do you actually start the process?

Forgiving yourself is not about bypassing the deeper emotions underneath—it's about understanding why you feel you don't deserve forgiveness. At the heart of that resistance is often *shame*, the silent weight that drowns out self-compassion.

Shame serves an essential protective purpose. As social beings, our survival has historically depended on acceptance by our tribe, family, and community. Connection with others is an innate desire and need. The terror that accompanies shame is deeply rooted in our survival instincts, as the younger parts of us fear rejection, isolation, or disconnection. This fear of exclusion often becomes internalized as beliefs like "I am bad" or "I am the mistake."

From a neurobiological perspective, shame activates a heightened parasympathetic state that can lead to immobilization and dissociation. This "freeze" response often manifests as a profound "need to disappear," resulting in physical symptoms like lightheadedness, nausea, ringing in the ear, rubbery legs, or a sense of detachment.

The classic "collapse posture" of shame—rounded spine, lowered head, downward gaze, and a slackened facial expression—reinforces feelings of helplessness and vulnerability. Researchers like Nina Bull and Bessel van der Kolk have observed how this physical state correlates with emotional experiences, emphasizing the interconnectedness of body and mind.

This "shameflammation" functions much like physical pain, serving as a protective mechanism. Just as pain prevents us from harming our bodies, shame prevents us from damaging our social relationships.

Chronic or unresolved shame can trap us in cycles of internalized self-blame and immobilization. Breaking this loop requires tools that ground us in the present, reconnect us to our bodies, and allow us to approach shame with compassion and understanding rather than fear or avoidance.

This exercise aims to help you identify, understand, and deconstruct the internalized shame that may be blocking your path to forgiveness of self. If you experience an activated response, remember to use any neuro tools that support your nervous system and bring you back to regulation.

Step 1. Create a Safe Space

Before diving into this emotional work, ensure you're in a safe, private, and nurturing environment:

- Find a quiet space where you can be alone and uninterrupted.
- Surround yourself with comforting objects like a blanket, a candle, or a favorite stuffed animal.

- Play calming music or sounds that help you feel grounded.

Step 2. Ground Yourself in the Present Moment

Start with a grounding exercise to connect to your body and the present:

- Sit comfortably and take deep breaths, inhaling for 4 counts, holding for 4 counts, and exhaling for 6 counts.

- Place one hand over your heart and the other on your stomach. Feel the rise and fall of your breath.

- Repeat silently or aloud: **"I am safe. I am here. I am ready to face this with compassion."**

Step 3. Explore Why You Feel Undeserving of Forgiveness

Shame often holds the key to why you feel forgiveness is out of reach. Use these prompts to gently uncover what lies beneath.

Write freely in the spaces provided, without judgment. Let the words flow, even if they feel messy or incomplete:

- **"What is the one thing I feel most ashamed of?"**

- **"What do I believe about myself because of this?"**

- **"Where did I first learn this belief?"**

Step 4. Uncover the Root of Shame

Shame often forms in childhood, tied to experiences where we felt:

- Rejected, or fear of being rejected for who we were.

- Punished for making mistakes.

- Blamed for things outside our control.

For example, you may realize you feel unworthy because a caregiver told you that making mistakes meant you were "bad." This was something you were taught, which means you can unlearn it over time as well. Reflect on whether that belief still serves you. Ask yourself and answer in the spaces below:

- **"When was the first time I felt this way?"**

- **"What message did I receive about myself in that moment?"**

- **"Was that message fair or true?"**

Step 5. Reframe the Story

Shame thrives in secrecy and black-and-white binaries. To loosen its grip, reframe the narrative and begin deconstructing it:

- Identify the critical belief driving your shame (e.g., "I'm a failure because I made a mistake"):

- Challenge its truth: **"Is it true that making a mistake defines my worth? What would I tell a friend who felt this way?"**

- Replace the belief with a compassionate one: **"I am human, and mistakes are part of growth. I am not defined by my worst moment."**

Step 6. Speak to Your Inner Child

Shame often originates in childhood wounds. Address your inner child directly:

- Visualize them standing before you, carrying the weight of their shame.

- Speak to them with compassion:
  - **"I see how much pain you're holding. It's not your fault."**
  - **"You were doing the best you could, and I love you exactly as you are."**

Imagine hugging and fully embracing your inner child or holding their hand as a symbol of your love and support.

Step 7. Offer Forgiveness

Now, gently begin the process of forgiving yourself. Forgiveness doesn't mean erasing the past but accepting it as part of your humanity. Say (or write) the following:

- **"I forgive myself for believing I was unworthy."**

- **"I forgive myself for carrying shame that was never mine to hold."**

- **"I am learning to let go of this shame so I can heal."**

- **"This shame no longer holds any power over me."**

- **"I am allowed to love myself more as I learn to let go of this shame a little more each day."**

Feel free to adapt these statements to fit your unique journey in the space below:

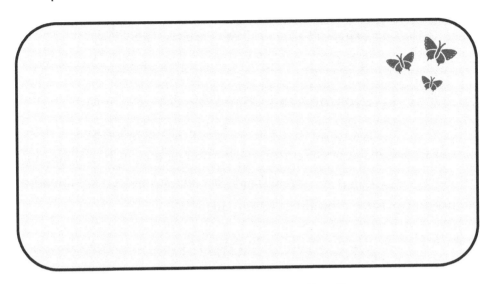

Step 8. Release the Shame Symbolically

Shame has an emotional weight, and releasing it through a symbolic act can feel deeply healing:

- **Write it down and destroy it**: Write your feelings of shame on a piece of paper, then tear it up, burn it (safely), or throw it away as a sign of release.

- **Wash it away**: Stand in the shower and imagine the water washing away your shame, leaving you cleansed and renewed.

- **Bury it**: Write your shame on biodegradable seed paper, bury it in the ground, and watch it grow into something new.

Step 9. Reinforce Self-Compassion

After releasing shame, focus on nurturing yourself. Speak affirmations to replace the negative beliefs shame created:

- **"I am worthy of love and forgiveness, no matter what."**

- "I am not my mistakes. I am my growth."

- "I am healing, one step at a time."

- "*Wanting* to heal also means that I am already healing."

Forgiveness is a journey, not a one-time event. You may need to revisit these steps as layers of shame surface over time. That's more than okay—it's part of the healing process. By shining a light on shame and extending compassion to yourself and your inner child, you're already taking a powerful step toward freedom and peace.

Remember, you are not alone in this process. Forgiveness is your birthright, and every step forward is an act of courage and self-love.

DAY 19

'Identifying Triggers'

This exercise can be used whenever you feel a trigger arising to recognize and work through personal triggers rooted in childhood trauma. It involves reflecting on past experiences, identifying the emotions and patterns connected to these triggers, and using neuro tools to regulate your nervous system through the triggers with parasympathetic upregulation.

Step 1. Recognizing Your Triggers

Reflect and Write: Take a few deep breaths and recall a recent moment when you felt suddenly emotional, reactive, or defensive. Write down:

- **What was the situation?** Describe it briefly.

- **What were your initial reactions?** Notice any immediate emotions (e.g., anger, sadness, fear) or physical sensations (e.g., tension, tightness, sweating, rapid heart rate).

- **What did you feel compelled to do?** Describe any actions or impulses (e.g., needing to leave, getting defensive).

Pattern Recognition Test

Identify whether this situation aligns with any of the following patterns. These are common patterns stemming from unmet childhood needs:

1. **Fear of Rejection or Abandonment**: Do you feel easily hurt, ignored, or anxious when someone doesn't respond as quickly or in the way you hoped?

2. **Hypervigilance**: Do you find yourself overly aware of other people's moods, body language, or tone of voice, especially when you sense tension?

3. **Need for Perfection**: Are you particularly reactive to criticism or extremely hard on yourself when making mistakes?

4. **Trust Issues**: Do you feel wary or suspicious of others' intentions, even in relatively safe situations?

5. **Difficulty with Boundaries**: Do you feel triggered when someone crosses a personal boundary, even if it's not done intentionally? Does it remind you of a possible boundary violation from your childhood?

Step 2. Mapping Triggers Back to the Root Cause

Trigger Pattern Analysis: Use this prompt to help you explore the origins of these patterns:

1. Think back to early childhood memories. When did you first feel emotions like fear, rejection, or distrust in close relationships?

2. What responses did you have to those early situations (e.g., shutting down, crying, hiding, people-pleasing)?

3. Note if there were specific people or repeated situations that made you feel this way.

Reflection Questions:

- Which of these childhood responses or feelings still affect you?

- How did these experiences shape the way you respond to similar situations as an adult?

Step 3. Regulating the Nervous System During Trigger Work

In moments when a trigger surfaces, it's common for your nervous system to enter a heightened state. Here are some neuro tools you can use to activate your parasympathetic nervous system to foster regulation and bring you out of dysregulation.

*1. 4-7-8 Breathing Technique *

- Inhale through your nose for a count of 4.

- Hold your breath for a count of 7.

- Exhale fully through your mouth for a count of eight. You can also hum to enhance activation.

- Repeat this cycle 3-4 times to calm the nervous system.

*2. Physiological Sigh *

This neuro tool helps regulate the nervous system, reduce stress, and increase **parasympathetic activation**. It is especially effective for quickly relieving feelings of anxiety or overwhelm.

Setup:

- Sit or lie down in a comfortable position where you can fully relax your body

- Ensure your back is straight if you're sitting and your shoulders are relaxed

*Make sure to still get a long, slow exhale to avoid hyperventilation!

Steps:

1. First Inhale:
   - Take a **deep, slow inhale** through your nose, filling your lungs to 80–90% capacity.

2. Second Inhale:
   - Immediately follow with a **shorter, quicker inhale** through your nose to fully expand your lungs to their maximum capacity.

3. Exhale:
   - Slowly exhale through your mouth with a long, controlled exhale.
   - Ensure the exhale lasts longer than the inhale.

4. Repeat:

- o Continue this cycle for 3–5 rounds or until you feel more relaxed and grounded.

Key Benefits:

- Quickly calms the nervous system by reducing heart rate and activating the parasympathetic response.

- Enhances oxygen exchange in the lungs for improved focus and relaxation.

- Easy to practice anywhere, making it a versatile tool for managing stress.

Pro Tip: Use this technique in moments of acute stress or as part of a daily relaxation practice.

---

*3. Dorsal Vagal Brushing *

This neuro tool gently stimulates the **dorsal vagal system**, promoting a sense of calm, safety, and connection. It can be especially useful for unwinding before sleep or as part of a self-care ritual.

Setup:

1. Select a Comfortable Object:
   - o Choose a brush or object that feels soothing and pleasant against your skin or clothing (e.g., a soft-bristle brush, textured fabric, or a smooth stone).

2. Find a Comfortable Position:
   - o Stand, sit, or lie down in a relaxed posture that allows easy access to the back of your body.

Cues for Success:

- Comfort First: Ensure that every movement feels good—adjust pressure, speed, or the object as needed.

- Small, Specific Movements: Think of the precision of brushing your teeth, focusing on small, deliberate strokes.

Steps:

1. Begin Brushing:
   - Use the object to gently stimulate the back side of your body.
   - Move in small circles or other patterns that feel good to you.

2. Target Key Areas:
   - Pay special attention to the back of your head and the back of your heart, areas connected to the vagal system.

3. Duration:
   - Spend a few minutes brushing, ensuring the movements remain soothing and intentional.

Modifications & Progressions:

1. Create a Ritual:
   - Use this exercise as a grounding ceremony, particularly before sleep, to signal safety and relaxation to your nervous system.

2. Explore Alternative Objects:
   - Experiment with objects that align with your belief system, preferences, or sensitivities (e.g., feathers, crystals, or textured tools).

3. Combine with Other Practices:
    o   Pair this exercise with soothing music/frequencies, dim lighting, or aromatherapy for a multisensory relaxation experience.

Key Benefits:

*   Stimulates the dorsal vagal pathway to promote deep relaxation and safety.

*   Encourages sensory exploration and self-soothing.

*   Can become a comforting, grounding ritual for transitions like bedtime.

Pro Tip: Use this tool as a regulation practice by focusing on the sensations and patterns of movement, bringing your attention fully into the moment to establish regulation and safety.

Step 4: Daily Practice & Tracking Patterns

Commit to repeating this reflection process any time you notice yourself becoming triggered. Gradually, you'll become more adept at identifying the origins of these triggers and responding with a regulation tool.

Optional Journal Prompts for Daily Reflection:

*   What trigger did I notice today?

*   Which nervous system tool helped me most?

*   How did I feel afterward?

Closing

Each time you notice and explore a trigger, remember that it's an opportunity to understand and reparent the younger version of you who felt hurt or unprotected. Be patient and gentle, acknowledging that this work unfolds gradually and that every step is valuable on the path to healing.

The goal is to better manage daily stressors and triggers, allowing us to approach uncomfortable conversations or situations with greater confidence as we continue to grow and heal. This helps prevent extreme emotional triggering and the loss of in-the-moment cognitive processing.

Give yourself grace, and remember to go at the pace that feels safest to you and your inner child.

DAY 20

'Side Quest'

Implement a required side quest once a week to excite/stimulate your inner child. Set aside time each week to explore activities that spark joy, curiosity, and creativity—cultivating an inner space of freedom and play that may have been missed in childhood. These side quests can help re-engage with a natural sense of wonder and self-expression.

Step 1. Choose Your Side Quest

Begin by brainstorming a list of activities that your inner child would love. Some ideas include:

- o Going to see a new movie or taking a class on something that intrigues you

- o Visiting a playground, interactive museum, or pet rescue

- o Going out to try a new coffee shop or restaurant

- o Learning or practicing a new hobby or skill

*Aim for activities that make you feel a sense of excitement or wonder, where your inner child is guiding you. *

Step 2. Commit to One Side Quest a Week

Each week, select one activity from your list. Schedule time for this activity as if it were an important appointment with yourself. Treat it as a "required" adventure to encourage commitment and consistency. Hold your boundaries on this "required" time.

Step 3. Set an Intention for the Activity

Before starting, take a moment to connect with your inner child. Set an intention such as, "Today, I am creating space for joy," or "I'm exploring for the sake of curiosity." Let this intention guide your experience.

Step 4. Engage Fully with the Activity

While on your side quest, allow yourself to be fully immersed. Notice how it feels to engage in this activity without judgment or expectation. Take mental notes (or journal afterward) about anything that feels playful, exciting, or comforting.

Step 5. Reflect on the Experience

Afterward, reflect on how the activity affected your mood, energy, and emotions. Did you feel moments of joy or calm? Did anything surprising come up?

Step 6. Celebrate and Repeat Weekly

Celebrate each completed side quest by acknowledging this weekly time dedicated to your inner child. Consider keeping a journal or scrapbook of these adventures, capturing memories, reflections, and even small mementos.

By making these side quests a part of your routine, you're giving your inner child a consistent space to be heard, seen, and expressed. Over time, this practice can nurture a more profound sense of freedom, imagination, and self-acceptance.

DAY 21

'Fearlessness'

Owning Your Opinions without Fear

This exercise aims to develop comfort in forming and expressing opinions, free from the fear of abandonment or rejection. It is designed to affirm your right to hold unique thoughts and perspectives without the guilt or shame you may have often felt as a child when trying to speak up for yourself or share your opinions.

Step 1. Safe Space Visualization

- Begin by sitting in a comfortable position. Close your eyes, take a deep breath, and visualize a safe, comforting place where your inner child feels completely protected and accepted. Our breathing exercise can also work for this step.

- Picture yourself as a child in this space, perhaps sitting beside a loving figure or surrounded by objects that bring peace and security. Allow yourself to linger here until you feel grounded and at ease.

Step 2. Journaling Your Opinions

- In this safe mental state, think about a recent event, conversation, or topic where you had trouble forming or sharing your opinion. Write down what your true feelings or thoughts were in the following spaces.

- As you write, remind yourself: "These are my thoughts, and I have the right to feel and think this way." Repeat this statement until it feels true, even if you have to gently challenge any guilt or doubt that comes up.

Step 3. Meet the Inner Critic with Compassion

- Write down any feelings of guilt or shame that arise when you imagine sharing your opinion. Notice if any specific memories or phrases come to mind:

- Address your inner critic with compassion, saying something like, "I see you're trying to protect me, but it's safe for me to express myself now. I don't have to fear being abandoned for being who I am."

Step 4. Rewrite the Narrative

- Reframe the experience by writing affirmations that support your right to have unique thoughts. Try phrases like:
    - "My opinions are valid and important."
    - "I am safe, even when others don't agree with me."
    - "I am allowed to have my own thoughts, and it doesn't make me unlovable."

Step 5. Practice with Small, Low-Risk Opinions

- Begin practicing sharing small, low-stakes opinions with others. For example, share your favorite movie, meal choice, or a recent experience. Focus on the feeling of speaking up without the fear of negative consequences.

- As you build confidence, gradually progress to sharing more personal thoughts.

Don't forget that you can use your neuro tools to help regulate your nervous system as you take steps toward creating a new internal sense of confidence when forming and expressing your own opinions.

Step 6. Daily Check-In

- Each day, spend a few minutes with this affirmation: *"I am safe in expressing myself, and I am worthy of acceptance and respect."*

- Reflect on the positive feelings that emerge when you start to own and honor your unique perspective.

Through this exercise, allow yourself to rewrite the internal script around guilt and shame, transforming it into self-acceptance and self-trust.

Over time, this will help you express yourself confidently without the weight of abandonment fears or letting others guilt you for having your own independent opinions and thoughts.

DAY 22

'IATAM'

Today's exercise is called the IATAM (pronounced "item"), which stands for **Intentionally Active Thought Awareness Method.**

The goal of this exercise is to start looking inward whenever you feel dysregulated in your nervous system and identify the origins of some of your thoughts. This can be used in any situation.

When a thought arises that feels scary, activating, or dysregulating, pause and ask yourself: *Where did this come from?*

- Was it triggered by something external?

- Are you potentially experiencing an emotional flashback that needs to be acknowledged, validated, and processed using a neuro tool for regulation?

- Did you recently eat something, and now your heart rate is speeding up because your body is working to digest it? Could this internal sensation be mistaken for anxiety?

- Are you feeling anxious but unsure why, especially about something mundane? Could your body have patterned anxiety as similar to the emotional experience of excitement, and now you simply need to retrain your nervous system to differentiate the two?

- Is a past childhood trauma, or fragments of an unprocessed trauma, resurfacing and asking to be acknowledged, validated, and processed?

There are many variables linked to internal dysregulation, which is why it's essential to cultivate a deepening relationship with your inner child. They may be communicating with you through your nervous system's *threat level outputs.*

Ideally, you want to develop the habit of using the IATAM as often as possible, but not for every thought, as this can quickly become overwhelming—especially if you already struggle with intrusive or spiraling thought patterns.

Start small and approach the process with curiosity. Ask your inner child if there's something they're trying to communicate to you. If it feels safe, try the video journal exercise or any others we've explored in this journal to help deconstruct and better understand the dysregulation within you.

The body remembers everything it has survived and lived through, and our role is to begin connecting the dots.

Over time, as you practice this method, you'll start to uncover and recognize your patterns and subconscious tendencies much more easily. Take it slow, and approach the situation with compassion and a sense of safety.

DAY 23

'Childhood Gaze'

This mirror-gazing exercise is designed to help you confront and begin deconstructing negative labels you may see in your reflection. Over time, these labels may have been embedded in your self-perception due to things people told you or through experiences of mistreatment, causing you to internalize these ideas as "truths" when they are not.

This exercise will help start the process of retraining your brain to see yourself with compassion and kindness instead.

Recognizing and releasing the labels and limiting beliefs tied to past experiences is essential while building a new, kinder relationship with your reflection and inner child.

Step 1. Set Up a Safe Space

- Find a quiet, comfortable place with a mirror where you won't be interrupted. If you like, light a candle or play gentle music to create a calming environment.

- Jot down any insights or emotions that arise in the following spaces.

Step 2. Set Your Intention

- Close your eyes and take a few deep breaths. Set a clear intention to approach this exercise with love and openness, reminding yourself that this is an opportunity to rewrite the old labels you may have carried for years.

- Acknowledge that you are here to show compassion to parts of yourself that may feel wounded or misjudged and are ready for healing.

Step 3. Begin Mirror Gazing

- Stand or sit in front of the mirror, making sure you can see your face and meet your own gaze.
- Look into your eyes gently, breathing deeply, and allowing any thoughts, emotions, or reactions to arise naturally without judgment.
- Remember, you can pause or stop at any time to regulate yourself if you start to feel overwhelmed or enter a heightened threat level.

Step 4. Identify Labels That Surface

- As you gaze, notice any automatic thoughts, labels, or judgments that arise. Do you see yourself as "not enough," "too much," "unworthy," or "undeserving"? **Write them down:**

- These labels may represent stories others imposed on you over time through words or actions. Allow them to arise, acknowledging that these are reflections of past pain, **not true reflections of who you are now.**

Step 5. Deconstruct the Labels

- For each label that surfaces, ask yourself, *"Where did this come from?" "Who told me this?" "Is this belief my own, or is it someone else's opinion?"*

- Try tracing each thought back to its source. For instance, if you think, "I'm not lovable," consider where or from whom you might have internalized this message. Is there an event, person, or experience tied to it? **Write it below:**

- Acknowledge that while these labels may feel true, they were born from past conditioning rather than an authentic understanding of yourself.

Step 6. Rewrite the Label with Compassion

- For every label you identify, gently counter it with a compassionate truth. If you catch yourself thinking, "I'm not enough," try affirming, *"I am enough exactly as I am right now."*

- Speak directly to yourself in the mirror with these new affirmations, countering each label with a statement of kindness. Practice repeating these compassionate truths out loud, allowing yourself to feel their impact.

- You can also use these new countering affirmations by writing them on your mirror to see every morning.

Step 7. Reframe Your Reflection

- With each affirmation, imagine that you're rewiring your brain to see a different version of yourself, one that is kind, lovable, worthy, and full of potential. Imagine these new words replacing the old labels, shifting how you perceive yourself.

- Visualize yourself shedding these past labels and emerging free, ready to embody the qualities of kindness, worthiness, and self-compassion.

Step 8. Record Any Insights or Patterns

- Once you feel complete, take a few moments to write down any insights or emotions that arose during the exercise. Note any recurring labels or patterns you identified, and record the compassionate truths you used to counter them.

- Write down your new affirmations and consider repeating these daily to help solidify a more positive and loving relationship with yourself.

New Countering Affirmations:

Aftercare and Practice

- **Grounding and Reflection**: This exercise may bring up strong emotions, so ground yourself afterward with a few deep breaths, stretching, or any neuro tools.

- **Daily Repetition**: To help solidify the new affirmations and retrain your brain, repeat these compassionate statements each time you see yourself in the mirror.

- **Celebrate Progress**: Recognize that each time you repeat this exercise, you're helping to create a shift in how you see yourself, a shift toward love, understanding, and compassion.

Over time, this exercise can help you peel away the labels that no longer serve you and replace them with the loving truths that honor your inner child. The more you do this, the more likely you'll find your reflection becoming a source of self-love and connection rather than criticism.

DAY 24

'Dance Like Nobody's Watching'

This exercise is about **embracing joyful self-expression through movement and allowing yourself to feel uninhibited.** Dancing to your favorite song can be a powerful way to connect with your inner child, build self-confidence, and release pent-up emotions.

Step 1. Set the Scene

- Choose a song (or a few) you love—something that brings out your joyful, uninhibited side and makes you want to get up and dance.

- Create a safe, private space where you can move freely without distractions. Dim the lights, light a candle, or do whatever helps you feel relaxed and in the moment.

Step 2. Let the Music Move You

- Start playing your favorite song and close your eyes. Allow the music to fill you, imagining you're in a space where no one can judge or interrupt you.

- Let your body move however it wants to. There's no "right" or "wrong" way, just notice how it feels to let go and follow the music.

Step 3. Feel the Joy of Self-Expression

- As you dance, remind yourself: *"This is my time to feel free and to express myself fully. I am safe, I am loved, and I am enough."*

- Imagine your inner child dancing along with you, letting go of any self-consciousness. Embrace the playfulness of simply being in the moment.

Step 4. Level-Up Challenge (Dance in Front of a Mirror)

- If you're ready to take it further, move in front of a mirror. Look at yourself while you dance, holding a soft, non-judgmental gaze.

- When self-critical thoughts arise, counter them with kindness, saying, *"It's just me and myself; nobody is watching, and I can vibe out however my body feels like it."*

  - Notice if you can let go of any tension or hesitation as you watch yourself move.

Step 5. Reflect and Ground

- Once the song ends, take a few deep breaths and place a hand on your heart. Thank yourself for showing up and letting go.

- Reflect on your thoughts: What did it feel like to move freely? Did any memories or feelings come up? How did you think about seeing yourself dance?

Close by writing one supportive affirmation below that captures your experience, such as: *"I am free to be myself—to move and dance exactly as I am."*

This exercise encourages self-acceptance, self-expression, and a joyful reconnection with your inner child. It's about embracing yourself with love and compassion, just as you would a friend dancing freely beside you.

It may take time to feel fully comfortable dancing unapologetically. Still, the more you practice this exercise, the easier it will become to silence the inner critic that may cringe at your authentic self-expression through somatic movement and dance.

DAY 25

'Sanctuary'

The objective of this exercise is to transform a space you call your own—whether it's a room, an apartment, or your entire home—into a sanctuary that reflects and celebrates you and your inner child. This practice helps you connect with the playful, expressive part of yourself, creating a space that brings comfort and joy every time you return home.

This process can be ongoing as you continually adjust and decorate your space. It becomes a form of self-expression, aligning with your most authentic self.

Step 1. Connect with Your Inner Child's Vision

- Sit quietly and close your eyes. Imagine your inner child is sitting with you. Take a moment to ask them: *"What would make you feel happy, comfortable, and safe in this space?"*

- Listen for their responses. They might bring to mind specific colors, items, or decorations that evoke joy or nostalgia.

Step 2. Reflect on Joyful Memories and Items

- Think back to items or themes from your childhood that brought you joy—a favorite color, pattern, or toy. Did you have a special blanket, a collection of something you loved, or a favorite poster?

- List a few things that make you smile, even just in memory. The goal is to incorporate elements that bring back that sense of childhood happiness and freedom.

Step 3. Begin the Transformation

- Now, look around your space and consider small changes you could make to reflect these joyful memories or preferences.

- Ideas could include adding playful art, putting up fairy lights, incorporating soft textures like blankets or pillows, or decorating with plants, toys, or childhood mementos. Focus on what makes you feel cozy, safe, and happy.

Step 4. Incorporate Meaningful Elements

- Consider the sensory elements of your space, such as scents, lighting, and sounds. Could you add candles with comforting fragrances, music that lifts your mood, or color-changing lights to create the perfect ambiance?

- Allow your inner child to guide the choices, selecting colors or decorations that they would love. Imagine this space as a refuge that captures their carefree, joyful essence.

Step 5. Personalize with Love

- Add at least one item that feels uniquely "you," symbolizing the bridge between your adult self and your inner child. It might be a journal, a piece of art you create, or a small statue or symbol of something that makes you feel loved and at home.

- Whenever you walk into this sanctuary, remind yourself: *"This space is here to nurture and honor all parts of me."*

Step 6. Sanctuary Time

- Make a habit of spending a few quiet moments each day acknowledging this space and reconnecting with your inner child. Notice how it feels to be in a sanctuary designed with both of you in mind.

- Reflect on the feelings that arise each time you enter. Allow any joy, nostalgia, or comfort to wash over you, and thank your inner child for helping you create this safe haven.

This sanctuary is more than just a decorated space; it's a reminder of your inner child's presence and your commitment to nurturing and honoring them every day. Let this space serve as a loving and joyful connection to who you've always been and who you are now choosing to become on this healing journey.

DAY 26

'Emotional Freedom Technique'

EFT Tapping with New Affirmations

Use Emotional Freedom Technique (EFT) tapping combined with new affirmations to connect with, validate, and soothe your inner child. EFT can help release stuck emotions, while affirmations can replace limiting beliefs with feelings of safety, love, and self-worth.

Step 1. Identify an Emotion or Belief to Address

Begin by identifying a limiting belief or painful emotion related to your inner child. Examples could include feeling "not enough," "invisible," or "unworthy." **Write in the space below:**

Step 2. Create a Set of New Affirmations

Choose or create affirmations that resonate with the specific belief or emotion. If you struggle with feelings of unworthiness, for instance, try affirmations like:

- o "I am enough, just as I am."

- o "I am safe to be myself."

- "I am loved, valued, and seen."

- "I deserve kindness and compassion."

Make these affirmations personal and uplifting, speaking to the inner child's need for love, safety, and acceptance.

Write them below:

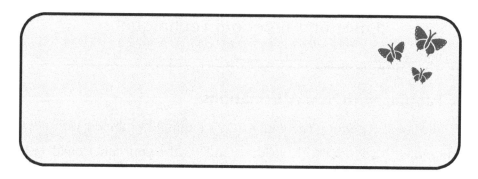

Step 3. Prepare for Tapping

Find a quiet, comfortable space where you can focus. Start by rating the intensity of the limiting belief or emotion on a scale from 1 to 10. This will help you assess your progress after the exercise.

Step 4. Begin the Tapping Sequence

Tap on each of the main EFT points repeatedly, moving through the sequence as follows:

1. **Karate Chop Point (outer part of the hand between the wrist and base of the pinky finger):** State your limiting belief/emotion. For example, "Even though I feel unworthy, I deeply and completely accept myself."

2. **Eyebrow Point (beginning of eyebrow closest to nose):** Transition to your new affirmation: "I am enough."

3. **Side of the Eye (the side furthest from the nose):** Repeat the affirmation, "I deserve to be seen and valued."

4. **Under the Eye**: "It's safe for me to feel loved and accepted."
5. **Under the Nose**: "I am gentle and kind to myself."
6. **Chin Point (under lips & above chin)**: "My inner child is safe and supported."
7. **Collarbone**: "I am free to feel joy and peace."
8. **Under the Arm (about 4 inches under the armpit)**: "I am whole, just as I am."
9. **Top of the Head (direct center of the top of your head)**: "I am worthy of love and acceptance."

Tap each point around 5–7 times as you repeat the associated affirmation.

Step 5. Repeat as Needed

Go through this tapping sequence two or three times, paying attention to any shifts in your feelings or intensity of the original belief.

Step 6. Reassess and Reflect

After completing the tapping, reassess the intensity of the original belief. Notice if it has decreased or shifted. Reflect on any new emotions, sensations, or insights that have come up.

Step 7. Journal Your Experience

Write below how you felt before, during, and after the tapping exercise. Note any positive changes in your thoughts or emotions and any inner-child messages or memories that surfaced:

Step 8. Commit to Daily or Weekly Practice

Consider practicing this tapping exercise regularly with new affirmations to reinforce inner child healing. Regular tapping can deepen self-acceptance, instill positive beliefs, and reduce limiting thoughts over time.

With this exercise, EFT tapping can become a powerful tool for healing, offering your inner child affirmations of love, safety, and worthiness through these points on your body.

DAY 27

'Nostalgia'

In today's exercise, we will revisit a movie, show, or book you loved as a child and reflect on how your feelings about it have changed over time. This process can reveal shifts in your perspectives, uncover memories, and help you reconnect with the younger version of yourself.

Step 1. Choose a Story from Childhood

Select a movie, show, or book that was significant to you in childhood. If it's been a while since you've revisited it, consider this a chance to see it with fresh eyes and an open heart.

Alternative Option: If you don't have specific media from your childhood, choose something age-appropriate that may have captured your attention at that time—like a classic animated movie, a storybook, or a fairy tale you know was popular when you were young.

Step 2. Set Aside Quiet Time

Find a quiet place where you can immerse yourself in this story. Allow yourself to engage with it fully, just as you might have done as a child.

Step 3. Notice and Reflect on Emotions

As you experience the story, observe your emotional responses. Do you feel joy, nostalgia, sadness, or even confusion? What do you think your younger self might have felt while watching or reading it?

Step 4. Compare Your Feelings

Reflect on the differences between how you felt about the story then and how you feel about it now. Consider questions like:

- What specific moments stood out then versus now?

- Did you notice new details or meanings you might have missed before?

- How did you relate to the characters and storyline differently?

- How has your sense of safety, excitement, or comfort in the story changed?

Step 5. Journal Your Experience

Write down your observations and reflections, capturing insights about your younger self and any new discoveries. You could also write a letter to your inner child about the differences between then and now, offering comfort or reassurance.

Step 6. Reflect on Your Inner Child's Needs

Based on this experience, consider if your inner child might have unmet needs revealed through this exercise. Is there a way you could provide those needs now, such as incorporating more joy, safety, or playfulness into your life?

This exercise encourages you to explore the distance traveled between your childhood self and who you are today. **By revisiting past media or themes, you can reconnect with the core of who you were, building compassion and understanding for the journey you've taken.**

DAY 28

'Climb a Tree'

The purpose of today's exercise is to reignite a sense of innocent wonder and curiosity for the world around you, stepping outside as your childhood self would—full of awe, curiosity, and open-hearted exploration.

Step 1. Choose & Enter with an Open Heart

- Choose a natural space to explore—a forest, beach, field, or garden. As you arrive, imagine you are seeing everything here for the first time without the need to label or understand it.

- Take a few deep breaths, feel your feet on the ground, and remind yourself, *"I am here to explore, to wonder, and to **simply be**."*

Step 2. Find the Magic in Small Details

- As you walk, slow down and notice things you might usually pass by. Run your fingers over a tree's bark and feel its texture. Pick up a leaf and look closely at its veins, colors, and shape. Take your time to observe without judgment or expectation.

- If something catches your attention, give yourself permission to pause and investigate. Let yourself feel as though you're discovering a little piece of magic. You are in no rush.

Step 3. Look at Nature Through Your Inner Child's Eyes

- Imagine you're seeing the world through the eyes of a young child—one who's endlessly curious and amazed by life's smallest details.

- Pick a small area around you to focus on, such as a patch of wildflowers or a puddle, and explore it deeply. Kneel down, touch, smell, and study every element, allowing yourself to be fully absorbed by the moment. What do you notice when you look at this piece of nature as a child would?

Step 4. Find a Sense of Adventure

- Look around and find something that might bring a sense of light-hearted adventure. Maybe there's a tree to climb, a small stream to cross, or a hidden path to follow.

- Let your inner child lead you with that innocent excitement, as though **you're on a quest to find something magical.** Feel the thrill of exploration, even if you're just taking a new route or walking barefoot in the grass.

Step 5. Let Go and Just Be

- Once you've explored, find a quiet spot to sit or lie down. Look up at the sky, noticing how vast and mysterious it feels, or watch the sunlight dance through the leaves above.

- Release any need to understand, analyze, or "do" anything. Allow yourself to be still, sinking into a state of awe and appreciation. Feel the wonder of simply existing in this world.

Step 6. Bring a Piece of Wonder Home

- Before leaving, choose one small item to bring back—a pebble, feather, or flower. Hold it in your hand and appreciate it as your inner child would, with a sense of awe for its uniqueness.

- Place it somewhere in your space as a reminder to embrace wonder and curiosity, keeping that sense of childlike bewilderment alive in your everyday life.

For many of us, stability and peace were scarce growing up. Exploring the outdoors, slowing down, and observing how nature and wildlife move effortlessly, without rushing, can serve as a foundational reminder: to begin flowing instead of forcing, we must first slow down and notice the intricate beauty and wonder surrounding us. Practice this exercise whenever your soul and inner child need their fire reignited.

DAY 29

'Self-Care'

After all the growth and healing you've cultivated on this journey, it's time to establish a foundation of self-care practices to support and protect your inner child moving forward.

These practices and boundaries you've been learning to set will serve as a lifelong toolkit to nurture your well-being.

While your self-care practices and boundaries may evolve as you grow, their core purpose remains constant: to ensure your inner child's safety and regulation in every situation. By prioritizing this, you empower the both of you to live with greater emotional regulation and resilience.

You'll begin to notice significant shifts over time—whether it's 3 months, 6 months, or a year. Triggers that once overwhelmed you will feel less intense, transforming from overwhelming waves to manageable ripples. These moments will serve as gentle reminders of how far you've come. What used to destabilize you will now feel like a small signal, one you can handle with ease because you've been training your nervous system to stay regulated as these things lose their power over you and come to the surface.

Your inner child will grow to trust you fully as the safe, supportive caregiver you've become. Together, you'll come to understand that while life can sometimes feel very uncertain or scary, you are now more than capable of showing up for those moments and moving through them with safety and regulation.

Your fear has now become a catalyst for exponential growth and healing.

Here are some ideas to inspire your list. Choose what resonates with you, and feel free to add your own:

1. **Daily Check-Ins**

   Spend a few moments each morning asking yourself, "What does my inner child need today?" This could be comfort, play, or reassurance.

2. **Nervous System Regulation**
   - Using any of your neuro tools whenever you feel dysregulated.

3. **Emotional Expression**
   - Journal your feelings, allowing yourself to process them without judgment.
   - Use creative outlets like drawing, painting, or singing to release emotions.

4. **Safe Boundaries**
   - Identify situations or relationships that feel draining or unsafe and set clear boundaries around them.

- Regularly review your "non-negotiable" and "negotiable" boundaries, ensuring they align with your needs.

5. Playful Exploration

- Dedicate time each week for activities your inner child loves—dancing, crafting, exploring nature, or watching a nostalgic movie.

6. Mindful Nourishment

- Choose foods that make you feel good physically and emotionally, and practice mindful eating.

- Stay hydrated and create rituals around meals that bring you joy.

7. Rest and Recharge

- Schedule "do-nothing" time to simply rest, nap, or daydream.

- Create a soothing bedtime routine that promotes deep, restorative sleep.

8. Affirmations and Mirror Work

- Write affirmations on your bathroom mirror or somewhere you'll see them daily.

- Look into your eyes in the mirror and remind yourself, "I am safe, loved, and capable."

9. Celebrating Wins

- Acknowledge even the smallest achievements in your healing journey, like handling a trigger differently or maintaining a boundary.

10. Connecting with Nature

- ○ Go for walks, breathe in fresh air, or spend time near water or trees to reset and recharge.

11. Community and Support

- ○ Surround yourself with people who respect your boundaries and encourage your growth.

- ○ Seek professional support, such as therapy or coaching, to guide your healing if that resource is available to you.

Your Task:

1. Create Your List

Write down at least 5-10 self-care practices that feel meaningful and supportive to you. Include specific examples of how you'll incorporate them into your routine.

2. Make It Visible

Place your list somewhere you'll see it daily—on your fridge, mirror, or desk—as a reminder of your commitment to yourself and your inner child.

3. Check In Regularly

Revisit your list every 3-6 months to reflect on how it's working for you. Adjust as needed to ensure it continues to align with your evolving needs and goals.

By anchoring yourself in these practices, you are creating a safe, nurturing environment for your inner child to thrive. You're teaching yourself that you are worthy of love, care, and stability, no matter what challenges arise.

DAY 30

'Finish Line'

Congratulations on completing your 30-day inner child healing journey! This is no small feat—it's a testament to your courage, resilience, and commitment to reclaiming the parts of yourself that longed for love, care, and understanding.

As you reach this final step, take a moment to honor the profound work you've done, the breakthroughs you've experienced, and the inner child you've welcomed back into your heart. Reflect on how far you've come, from uncovering hidden wounds to embracing joy, and recognize the strength it takes to walk this path of healing.

This final exercise is an opportunity to celebrate your progress, acknowledge the raw power of your journey, and set intentions for the future with clarity and self-compassion.

Healing is not about striving for perfection but about growth, connection, and embracing your wholeness. You've proven to yourself that you are capable of transformation, and now it's time to carry forward everything you've learned into a future rooted in confidence, joy, and unconditional self-love.

Step 1: Reflect

Find a quiet, comfortable space where you can sit with your thoughts and feelings. Write down your reflections on the following prompts:

- **Before the Journey**: How did you feel about yourself and your inner child before starting this journal? What was your relationship like with your inner child?

- **During the Journey**: Which exercises resonated with you the most? Which ones were the most challenging? What did you discover about your inner child along the way?

- **After the Journey**: How do you feel now compared to how you felt 30 days ago? How has your relationship with your inner child evolved?

Step 2: Celebrate Your Growth

This journey has been an act of love, courage, and dedication to yourself. Celebrate your achievements in a way that feels joyful and meaningful.

Ideas for Celebration:

- Revisit one of your favorite exercises from this journal and do it today.

- Plan a special outing or activity that lights up your inner child's soul.

- Create a tangible keepsake (a piece of art, a photo, a written letter) that symbolizes your growth.

Step 3: Commit to Your Healing

Your healing doesn't end here, as it's a lifelong practice of honoring your needs and nurturing your inner child. Write a letter to yourself and your inner child, committing to continue using these tools whenever needed. Include affirmations like:

- "I am capable of handling triggers with compassion and strength."

- "I will prioritize joy, creativity, and self-care."

- "I will honor the boundaries and practices that protect and nurture my inner child."

- "I am healing, growing, and becoming the person my inner child always needed."

Keep this letter somewhere safe to revisit whenever you need reassurance or inspiration.

Step 4: Live Authentically

You are now equipped to navigate life's stressors and triggers with resilience, love, and grace. From this moment forward:

- Practice these exercises whenever you and your inner child need them.

- Trust in the healing you've done and the strength you've built.

- Seek out what brings you joy, lights your soul on fire, and nourishes the connection with your inner child.

Take one final moment to look at yourself in the mirror, truly see your reflection, and say: "I am proud of you. I see you. I love you."

Feel the depth of those words as they reach the heart of your inner child, a child who longed for recognition, safety, and unconditional love. Know that you are now the caretaker, protector, and nurturer of that child, and you've done the work to begin creating a life where you both can thrive.

Go forth with confidence, joy, and love, carrying the tools and lessons you've gathered here. Embrace the freedom to set boundaries, to play, to express your truth without shame, and to move through life as your most authentic self. You are whole, worthy, and enough—just as you are, and you always have been.

Remember, healing is a journey, not a destination. Remind yourself that each step you take is an act of courage and self-compassion.

When challenges arise, reconnect with the moments of healing and breakthroughs you've experienced on this journey. Draw strength from the raw power you cultivated by allowing yourself to feel what needed to be felt and validating the pain that was once silenced. These moments are your proof of resilience, courage, and the love you've reclaimed for yourself.

You are not alone. You are deeply loved—by yourself, by the parts of you that are healing, and by your future self, who is so excited to meet you. You've got this.

I'm sending you all the love and light energy
-Cody

Closing Letter

'The Seeds'

I was given seeds to plant when I was younger.

Seeds that were meant to help me grow—or so you said.

But I wasn't shown or told what they would grow into.

I was simply told to plant them, to trust without knowing, and to follow without question.

I wasn't allowed to ask why.

Questioning things was dangerous around you.

It was met with anger, with silence, or worse.

I remember how you dropped the seeds, carelessly.

Letting them scatter on the floor as if they didn't matter.

As if *I* didn't matter.

You didn't hand them to me gently, with care or love.

You made me kneel down to pick them up.

A gesture that felt less like a gift and more like a punishment.

Like you were looking down on me.

I didn't understand what I'd done to deserve the weight of your indifference.

But it reminded me how small it made me feel.

That I was insignificant.

That I existed only to fulfill your expectations.

I hesitated to reach for the seeds.

Not because I didn't want to grow, but because I didn't feel safe.

Not with you standing over me.

Not with the shadow of your anger looming in the air.

Maybe it was because I remembered the times you hurt me.

The sting of your words.

The weight of your hands.

The crushing silence that followed.

I thought you loved me.

Or maybe I just needed to believe it.

Because without that belief, where would I have found my worth?

But the seeds—

The seeds became the love I searched for in you but never found.

The person I might have been if only I did.

If only someone had knelt beside me.

And showed me how to plant them.

How to water them.

How to grow.

As I look back now,

I realize those seeds were never about growth.

They were about control.

About bending me into the shape you wanted me to take.

But I have a garden now.

A garden of my own making.

A garden that is safe.

And though it's taken years to learn with much pain to be processed, I now know how to plant seeds with unconditional love—

For myself.

And I promise my younger self this:

I will *never* make you kneel again.